I Heard You Speak to Me

ALEX RUSSO

Fulton Books
Meadville, PA

Published by Fulton Books 2023

ISBN 979-8-88731-841-7 (paperback)
ISBN 979-8-88731-842-4 (digital)

Printed in the United States of America

To Sarah, who inspired me to write this book
To my mom, my daughter, Robert, Lili and E. Lambie

PREFACE

Have you ever heard God talk to you or thought you did? Maybe you don't believe in God. Perhaps, to you, it's just a "higher power."

How do you feel about all the trite phrases regarding life, faith, and mystery? Expressions like the ambiguous "Things happen for a reason." I've wondered about this one often. Maybe they do. Then we have the trite, often passive quips of "God works in mysterious ways" and "When one door closes, another opens." They're a dime a dozen. But what if it's all nonsense? What if…life just happens?

Well, here's my account of a life that swerved through detours, pain, and resilience. See for yourself.

E. Lambie

February 1989

The Start of It All

I used to attend lectures back in the eighties from a wonderful author, mystic, and spiritual healer, Betty Bethards. She believed in God, which was unique for this type of content, so it piqued my interest. She was convinced that we arrived on earth in our "little earth suits" and were given life lessons a total of three times each until we got them all correct. Once we completed them all, we'd then spend eternity in heaven with God. Sounded like a pretty good deal to me.

My birth name was Maria Adeline DeLucca, but everyone called me Addy. I was named after my grandmother, Maria Luciano. Maria was fully Italian, but my mother loved the Spanish name Adeline because the translation meant "noble." So here I am. I was raised a devout Catholic and attended a Catholic school. During that time, I was taught the ways of the devout. Every Friday, I would sit in the small, dark confessional booth, confessing all my sins to a priest. Then like clockwork, the priest would offer my penance and pray with me to complete the full cycle. The prayers were routine. *Our Father…three Hail Marys… Amen.*

I did this every Friday, no matter what. I remembered years earlier when I was eight years old, standing in line behind my classmates, awaiting my turn to unveil evil ways. I'd stand there, searching my memories for the last sins I had committed. This was particularly hard for a young child. What could I have possibly done that would be deemed so terrible it required full penance and forgiveness in order to protect my soul? There were times that I chose to make up sins just to stay relevant to the task at hand.

"I lied to my mom once and my dad twice," I would say.

Then the gruff voice on the other end of the grate would grant my penance, and I'd return to the pew and throw out the prayers for the absolution of my phantom errors. Looking back, I wondered, *Was it also a sin to lie about lying?* Next question.

Among the more challenging aspects of my faith were the dietary restrictions during Lent. During the forty days of sanctity, we couldn't eat meat every Friday. It was a struggle at times. Here I was, at a basketball game, when I bought a hot dog. Not entirely thinking through this, with an empty stomach, I went to take a bite. Then remembered, *It's Lent!* Now knowing it's Lent, it's a sin if I ate it. But if I threw it away, I was being wasteful, and that's a sin too! Decisions. *Which one was I willing to share at the confessional booth next week?*

These, among others, were the challenges I faced as a young child growing up in the Catholic faith. Though confusing at times and anxious at others, through it all, my commitment and self-awareness contributed to the strong woman I was today. The burden was heavy, but I was grateful for the benefits.

My parish was in a small town, often called a hippie town or better yet, *hippie's ville.* This was probably because Janice Joplin lived near there at one point in her life. I loved it. It was small, and our priest, Father Al, was a lovely, down-to-earth man. He gave beautiful homilies and was progressive enough even to bring in outsiders to speak at times. One Sunday, he had asked the Little Sisters of the Poor to share at our service. They were (and still are) a wonderful group of Catholic women devoted to caring for the impoverished elderly. Their core belief was that no one should die alone. With their organization, the elderly and dying were cared for with love and dignity, regardless of wealth or status.

When they visited, they asked for volunteers to help them with their cause. This struck a chord in me. *Why shouldn't I volunteer?* It made perfect sense. But there was one problem: I knew myself too well. If I decided to stay local and assist, I'd eventually cancel when something better came. I was like that for most things. But this was something different. I have always admired Mother Teresa and how she cared for the sick and dying. I firmly committed that this was going to be my mission. I just needed to figure out how.

Now remember, this was the eighties. The internet wasn't what it was today. It was all but inaccessible to most and not nearly as equipped to answer the millions of questions we ask it. So I was hard-pressed to find a way to reach out to this speaker. I knew she was in Calcutta, India, but I had no clue how to find her. I decided to ask Father Al. He knew everything. Sure enough, he had an address where I could write to her. I wrote her a note explaining how I wanted to volunteer with her. Three weeks later, I received an application. The journey was starting. *Could this be happening?*

Then it dawned on me: *What was I thinking?* I had a six-year-old daughter and a full-time job! *How could I possibly consider leaving?* I knew my former husband wouldn't be happy with this plan. Also, I knew that you didn't simply fly across the country just to stay for a week. In fact, the volunteer requirements were longer commitments. My head was spinning. *What was I thinking? Why do I even feel compelled to do something like this?*

When I told my friends and family my idea, they were excited for me. Though hopeful and supportive, they, too, wondered how I could pull it off. One of my closest friends, Frankie, was into psychics and suggested that I see her favorite. She assured me that she was very good. My appointment was set up for the next week.

As I sat with the psychic, she told me I had a karmic debt to pay, and this was why I might have been drawn to this type of service. She also informed me I was *not* going to Calcutta. Instead, I would go to a different place and receive a letter in the mail just before leaving that would reaffirm this location.

Karmic debt? I was not even supposed to believe in past lives or karma! Let's just say I was skeptical.

Around this time, I also approached my employer. I had a great job and bosses I really appreciated working for. Unfortunately, that conversation didn't go as well as the others. My leaders were excited for me about my adventure but couldn't promise me employment upon my return. This was such a blow. I had been with them for nearly eight years, so it goes without saying that I had expected more.

Nevertheless, I felt I had to do this. I truly believed that the twists and turns were simply tests from a higher power, and I didn't want to fail. There was no turning back.

When I finally informed my former husband, he wasn't too keen on the idea. The thought of me leaving him with our six-year-old for an extended time without support was rather unsettling. Thankfully, my wonderful mother stepped up to the plate and was willing to help in my absence. This put his fears at ease but didn't settle the heartache I felt at the thought of leaving my baby girl for nearly two months. Yes, she was my *baby girl*—even at six!

Once everyone was informed and all the right parties made aware, next came preparing my travel plans. I had a beloved travel agent named Kathy, and I was very excited to have her help me put together a great trip to Calcutta.

When the time came to sit with her, her immediate reaction was, "Why on earth would you want to go there? That is the filthiest place on the earth!"

Not the warm embrace I had hoped for.

But she wasn't done. "No! I am not going to let that happen. I am going to put you in contact with my cousin, Jan, a flight attendant. She and her crew did some veer work for *Mother Theresa's Missionaries for Charity* in Kathmandu, Nepal. That's where you want to go."

It appeared that my mind was made for me in a flash (and because I trusted Kathy). I met with Jan, who gave me the contact information for a Father Michael in Kathmandu. Apparently, he said mass daily for the Missionaries of Charity (Mother Teresa's order). The sisters worked along the Pashinath River in Kathmandu, caring for the sick and dying. I immediately mailed him to ask if he could put me in contact with Mother Teresa's sisters to see if I could volunteer for them in Nepal.

It seemed like an eternity had passed before I heard back from him. In the meantime, I stayed busy with my preparations. I got all my vaccination and passport and even began arranging for my plane ticket to Calcutta just in case Kathmandu was not an option. I had no idea whether any of this was going to work or not. Throughout it all, I kept thinking about what the psychic had told me: *I would receive something in the mail a few weeks before I was supposed to leave.* But I still didn't even know when I was going to leave!

Finally, I received a letter from Father Michael. Come to find out, he was a Maryknoll Missionary from Kentucky serving his time in Nepal. In the letter, he offered me a place to stay in his House of Hospitality. The psychic was right! How did she know? Regardless, it was time to change my ticket from Calcutta to Nepal.

Suddenly things were falling into place. It was all happening so fast! I started to get nervous. I was going to a country where I didn't even speak the language (Nepalese), and I was leaving my six-year-old daughter for more than a month. *What was I thinking?* But it was happening. In three weeks, I'd be going on a new, scary journey of the unknown. *Time to start preparing.*

Somehow the local newspaper got wind of the news and asked if they could do an interview. Of course, I agreed. They came to my employer to do the interview. Everyone was so excited to see them arrive an even someone to take my photo! I was featured on the front page. "Local Town Gal Travels Across the Country to Volunteer for Mother Teresa".

To help close the distance some, I began recording myself reading my daughter her bedtime stories. Just in case she missed me, I wanted her to have something that she could listen to from me. Perhaps the most challenging part of my preparations was knowing I had to say goodbye to her.

I packed a huge duffel bag with coloring books, construction paper, a stapler, scissors, and anything I could think of that might be entertaining for these people I had never met before. I tried to put myself in the place of a caretaker. What kind of things would they want to do? I also packed my tape recorder. I wanted to record the sights and sounds of this strange country I had never been to.

The week before I left, I visited my church alone to light a candle and pray for God's guidance. I also wanted to reconfirm that I was doing the right thing. The church was empty and quiet. I smelled the strong scent of burning incense. Oh, how I loved that smell. I bowed my head in reverence when I felt a hand on my shoulder in the middle of my prayers.

Slightly startled, I turned to see who it was. It was Father Al.

As if he was reading my thoughts, he whispered, "Don't worry. Everything will be all right. You are doing the right thing." He lifted a finger and added, "Can you wait a minute? I have something I want to give you."

"Yes, of course."

When he returned to the church, he reached into his pocket and pulled out an envelope and handed it to me.

"We wanted you to have this. We heard about your employer not promising you a position when you return. It isn't much, but it should help."

Tears rolled down my face as I got up and hugged him.

Then the dam burst, and sobbing, I said, "Thank you."

I whispered goodbye and walked away from this kind, gentle soul. With the envelope in hand, I got in my car and struggled to regain my composure. The envelope wrinkled in my grasp as I clenched it while dabbing my eyes with a Kleenex. Father Al had told me, "It wasn't much," but it *was* something. And he owed me nothing. I opened it up, and to my surprise, it was a check for $500. I was overwhelmed. The dried tears were quickly replaced with a new round of emotion as I laid my head back on the seat and closed my eyes before finally heading back to my preparations and the restless wait until I was off to Kathmandu.

The entire drive home, I kept asking God, *What are You doing to me? What is my lesson here?*

April 1989

Humble Servant

The day finally came, and I said goodbye to my family, friends, and my adorable daughter, Nicole. This wasn't easy. There were many tears.

Once aboard the plane, I settled into the long flight. Because of the distance, there were many transfers, and of course, being the eighties, we didn't have rolling suitcases—so I kept asking myself, *Why on earth did I bring two huge duffel bags with me?*

In total, the trip to Nepal was approximately twenty-four hours. At one point, I had to transfer to Bangkok. That was a long stretch. Plenty of time to stew in all the emotions I was feeling. Once I arrived, I retrieved my two huge duffel bags and had to carry them to the next flight for the remainder of the trip, kicking myself for the heavy luggage again. *Why did I pack so much for a mission trip to Kathmandu?* Here in Bangkok, I met a good-looking man who assisted me by carrying one of my duffel bags across the airport. After casual small talk, he told me his name was Patrick.

"Just call me Pat," he added.

"Thank you, my name is Adeline, but just call me Addy." I thanked him for his help, and he returned with a beautiful smile highlighting his blue eyes and gorgeous, long blond hair. He was tall and slim, physically fit, and *very* handsome. *Wow, I wonder where he's going.*

After a somewhat aggravating twenty-four hours of travel, I finally arrived in Nepal. I was exhausted. When I exited the plane,

"

I was immediately met with some very interesting (to say the least) smells. People were speaking in a language I had never heard before, and I was swept up by the hustle and bustle of people holding up signs I couldn't even read. To call it a whirlwind would be an understatement. In the midst of it all, there I was, holding these two obnoxiously heavy duffel bags, alone in a foreign country. As I paused and looked aimlessly, someone approached me and offered to rescue me. Who? Well, the mysteriously handsome man, Pat, of course!

"Hey, can I help you?" We both laughed.

Twice now, we ran into each other! Well, he was also in Nepal. Just like me. *Boy, was I lucky!* Before I knew it, I heard another voice yelling, "Addy!" waving his hands from across the airport. When I finally found the body that matched the voice, I saw an adorable man with the biggest smile I had ever seen.

He approached me and bowed his head with a soft, "Namaste, welcome to Nepal. I'm Father Michael."

I replied with a warm hello and then turned around to catch another sight of my savior. But by then, Pat had disappeared, and before I knew it, Father Michael was helping me with my bags and escorting me out of the airport.

The streets were full of cars, motorbikes, and bicycles. There was so much noise. I had no idea what my housing was going to be like, but if Father Michael's welcoming smile was any indication of my accommodations, I wasn't concerned. Expecting something humble, I was caught off guard when I arrived at the house. It was a beautiful gem compared to its surroundings in Nepal. My bedroom was small but clean. There was no running hot water in the house, but that was okay as it was pretty hot there. As I washed the trip off in the cold water, I realized that there was a lizard living in my shower. I thought, it *Looks like I've met my roommate!*

Father Michael informed me that there were three meals provided each day. One day a week, there would be meat with the meal (chicken). Beef was never eaten in Nepal. Cows were considered sacred, at least by the Hindus. The three meals were *dal bhat*, which basically was lentils and rice. Three times a day: lentils and rice. If you're not a fan of lentils and rice, then you are in trouble. As far as the meat I was promised, to this day, I never saw any of it. Every once in a while, we were fed a piece of bread with peanut butter. *This became a delicacy!*

The dress code was strict. I could only wear long pants or a long skirt, and I could wear a shirt, but it couldn't be sleeveless.

A woman was never to show her whole arm. And if I ever went into a temple, I always had to remove my shoes before entering.

Father Michael also educated me on the caste system in Nepal. Since I was going to be working with the sick and dying, it was important for me to understand how society was structured. He informed me that there were four traditional caste systems: Brahmins (priests and teachers), Kshatriyas (rulers and warriors), Vaishyas (merchants and cultivators), and Shudras (servants). While he was explaining this to me, he paused and took a big swallow. It was then that he informed me I would be considered a servant, the lowest of the caste.

On my first official day, I began at 6:00 a.m. by attending mass with Father Michael. It was here I met the sisters with the order Missionaries of Charity. I was relieved to hear from Father Michael that they spoke English. When I was introduced to them, the relief was quickly replaced with panic as I realized even though they spoke English, I couldn't understand a word they said. Their Indian accents were heavy. It sounded like they were singing a song every time they spoke—and I didn't know the lyrics. *This was going to be an interesting experience.* Regardless, they were very hospitable and warm. They made sure to make me feel right at home.

One morning, the sisters asked Fr. Michael and me if we wanted to stay for breakfast, and of course, we obliged. Much to my surprise, it wasn't *dal bhat*. It was a hard-boiled egg and white rice mixed in a yellow sauce. I had never tasted anything like it. I loved it! It was such a welcomed change.

The sisters saw my face light up. "Do you like it, Adeline?"

"Yes, what is it?"

Sister Mary answered, "Indian food, curry." *Hmm… I've never heard of this.*

It was 1989, so diverse food was rather scarce where I was from.

After mass ended, I followed them to the Pashupatinath temple, which sat directly behind the shelter where I would begin caring for the sick and dying. Right beyond the shelter was the Bagmati River.

My first job on site was cleaning out the toilets. Now let's pause. These were not your normal toilets. Essentially, it was a cement hole in the ground. My job was to carry water from the river that I then flushed down the hole. After that, I would use a brush and clean it out. The fun didn't stop there, though. Once the hole was "clean," then I went to task, scrubbing the floors around it. *Humble servant.*

My second job was laundry. I'd carry the dirty clothes down to the river and wash them with stones and some type of bar soap. After they were "clean," I'd carry them back up to the shelter and hang them on ropes that were stretched as clotheslines to air-dry.

The third job was bathing the patients and emptying bedpans. They were so thin and frail. It was heartbreaking. Other patients weren't too bad, but I could tell it was very embarrassing for them for me to assist them this way.

After that came feeding the patients. It sounded simple enough, but the hardest part was trying to convince some to let you feed them. I asked the sisters why some of them wouldn't let me feed them. She informed me that they considered me such a lower caste that I was worse than even a servant. Basically, I was beneath them. They needed to be fed, but they didn't want to be helped by the likes of me. Once again, *humble servant.*

My fifth and final job was assisting with medications. The meds were delivered from all over the world and donated to the Missionaries of Charities. Volunteers would sit around the table, and the sisters would divide the medication for us according to the language we spoke. We would each then take turns telling the sisters what each bottle read, and they would organize them in their dispensary by the label. I thought, *I wish I knew what to do with all these medicines.* It was then that a light bulb went off in my head. Holding that medicine bottle in my hand suddenly felt *right* to me. Little did I know that a seed had been planted in my brain. Week one wrapped, and I muscled my way through my jobs. When it was all said and done, I began to feel more comfortable with my routine.

In week two, I decided to bring out some of the things from my duffel bag to see if the patients would mind some art projects. It was a success. They loved them! We decorated their beds and brightened up the place. The patients had so much fun. I pulled out my tape recorder, sang a little song, and then played it back to them. They were fascinated by this technology. Before I knew it, patients were gathered all around me, wanting to talk into "this machine." By this time, I had learned to speak a little Nepali. It was basic, but I could manage enough to ask them each their name and then tell them mine. For some reason, they couldn't say Adeline, my given name, which was good because I preferred Addy. The sisters, on the other hand, preferred to call me by my given name. The arts and crafts and, of course, the tape recorder, made *Addy* very popular that night!

I was receiving mail regularly from family and friends back home in the US. I was also allowed one phone call a week. I chose every time to hear my sweet daughter Nicole's voice.

The weeks flew by, and I grew to love my patients. One day a frantic woman approached me and pulled me to a patient's bedside, where she motioned for me to feed him. I left there and hurried toward the sisters to talk about him. I learned he had not eaten in three days. The woman was begging me to try and get him to eat. I decided to mash up some cookie-type biscuits with goat milk and made a paste. I attempted to feed him much like I did my daughter when she was a baby. After many failed attempts, he finally took a small bite. Then he took another and another. Before I knew it, he finished the whole bowl. His eyes snapped open and stared straight into mine. In an odd, almost mystical way, it felt like there was a string that connected us together. The look in his eyes seemed to softly say "Thank you." I had never experienced anything like this before. It was as if time stood still when he looked at me that way. After he finished, the woman—who I later found out was his sister—began screaming something in Nepalese. She bear-hugged me and then put her arms around both of us.

I left the river that day asking myself, *I wonder if that was my Karmic debt the psychic was talking about?* The walk back toward the House of Hospitality that day, through the narrow, busy streets of

Nepal, suddenly felt more familiar than it had before. I began to feel a sense of homecoming. I couldn't understand what anyone was saying around me, but I felt like I had just walked into my own backyard, surrounded by people I'd known for years. It was such an overwhelming yet confusing feeling.

When I got home to the residence, I told Father Michael about my experience. I was very perplexed by it all. Being raised such a strict Catholic, it was ingrained in me not to believe in past lives or karmic energy. I told him what the psychic had shared with me about my *karmic debt.* I explained to him that in my short time in Nepal, I had never been exposed to so many different religions. *How can there be so many in this world when I was raised to only trust my own?* For the first time in my life, I was in the minority.

Now think about this. Here I was confessing all this personal confusion and spiritual discovery to a priest! But this wasn't like the confessions from when I was eight years old.

With profound wisdom and even greater grace, he softly responded, "If you think you need more than one life to learn everything, then I think you are probably right."

I was floored by the answer, but he wasn't done.

He added, "Don't you think our God is so wonderful that He can take on many forms to appeal to all types of people?"

Wow. What an amazing priest to take something so complicated and intricate and put it into terms that were simple to understand. He instantly put me at ease. I went to bed that night feeling as if a massive burden had been plucked from my shoulders.

The next day I returned to the river, anxious and excited to find out how my patient was doing. I ran down the hall to greet him, but when I arrived, I found his bed empty.

One of the sisters approached me and softly whispered, "Adeline, he is with God now."

"What!" I was heartbroken. "He was doing so well! He was eating again! How did this happen?"

The sister calmly responded, "You gave him his last meal, and God is very pleased with you."

I sat down on his bed and cried.

Later, I ran down to the river to watch his cremation. Hindus are cremated on the banks of the river. According to tradition, the body is dipped three times into the river prior to the final act. The chief mourner (usually the first son) who lights the funeral pyre must take a bath in the holy river water immediately after cremation. I could smell the stench of burning flesh. It wasn't a pleasant smell. This definitely was not the way I wanted my day to start. I finished my chores with a heavy heart. I left early that day to go to the Consulate before escaping back to my room for the night. *God works in mysterious ways.* He sure did, and this was one of those mysteries.

Every three weeks in Nepal, you must go to the Consulate and renew your visa. While standing in the long line, I heard, "Addy!"

Somewhat shocked to hear this, I quickly turned around to see who had called me. There he was. The devilishly handsome Mr. Blue Eyes. Pat.

My heart started beating fast. I couldn't believe my timing on this trip. It seemed like every time I was anywhere outside of the mission, there he was.

He spoke again, "Hey, do you want to grab some tea and catch up after we finish here?"

I blurted out somewhat too quickly, "Yes, of course!"

When we finished with our visas, we sat over tea and talked. He went on to tell me how he had been trekking all over Nepal and was thinking of going to Chitwan National Park. He asked if I might want to tag along with him. I was conflicted. I had come to do a mission. But here was this handsome guy asking me to explore the Chitwan National Park with him. I told him I would think about it. I asked if he would swing by the House of Hospitality the next day to meet Father Michael. For some reason, I felt I needed Father Michael's approval to do this.

I went home and told Father Michael about Pat and his invitation.

He immediately said, "Oh, you have to go! That place is amazing. You have been working really hard these past three weeks, Addy. You deserve a little time off."

Pat came by the next day and met Father Michael, receiving his approval. We left early the next morning, taking a sixty-mile bus ride to get to the park. When we arrived, we decided to share a cabin. It was less expensive, and it came with separate beds, so it made sense.

On the first day, we went on elephant rides through the jungle. It was beautiful. We were in the Terai lowlands of south-central Nepal. There were Bengal tigers, crocodiles, and so many bird species that I had never seen before. It was unlike anything I had ever experienced in my life.

The next day, we hiked through the jungle, looking for rare one-horned rhinos. This was a bit scarier. Our tour guides had failed to inform us that if they came near our group, we'd have to climb up a tree! It was exhilarating but also somewhat petrifying. There were several close calls, and of course, Pat came to my rescue more than once, helping me get up the tree. That night we experienced traditional fire dancing and drums. We ate the food and had a little too much Raksi (Nepali alcohol). It was our last night there, so we lived it up.

We went back to the room and climbed into our separate beds. We lay there in the dark, talking about our experiences of the past two days. After a few moments, there was a quick silence.

Suddenly, Pat said, "Addy, can we just hold each other?"

I paused and thought about it. I was the good Catholic girl, right? Wouldn't this be a sin? *Oh, man, why did I have to grow up Catholic?* This darn *sin thing* was maddening sometimes. My thoughts were racing. *He's so cute. What harm would it be to just hold each other?*

Finally, after a brief few seconds of moral wrestling, I declined. I could tell he was frustrated, but after a heavy sigh, he told me he understood. But I couldn't stop thinking about it.

After a few more moments, I added, "Okay, you promise just to hold each other?"

"Yes, I promise."

He slipped into my bed and wrapped around me, his body warm. He caressed my neck softly, and I turned around to face him. We kissed for the first time. I felt like I was in high school again. It seemed like we kissed for hours. Every time we'd come up for air, we'd talk about life, our failed relationships, and life experiences. He told me about his experience with smoking peyote in the desert during some sort of spirit walk. He said he felt like he was always searching for something he felt he was missing in his life. It became a magical night of pouring our souls out to each other. Before we knew it, the sun came up, and we had to catch our bus.

The bus ride home wasn't so great. Somehow, we both got dysentery. More than likely, it was from the water we drank at the camp. By the time we got back to Kathmandu, we were both very sick. Father Michael welcomed us into the house. We took turns holding each other's hair while we vomited and held cold washcloths to each other's necks. *Now talk about bonding!* Father Michael fetched both of us antibiotics. He allowed Pat to stay in my room on the other bed. I think he knew nothing would happen because we were too sick! By day three, we were much better. It was also the day Pat was scheduled to head back to Seattle.

His cab arrived quickly the next morning.

As Pat hurried out the door, he yelled back, "Wait, we didn't exchange addresses!"

The cab driver kept honking as I quickly jotted down my address for him. There was no time to get his. He promised he would write and visit. I had a feeling that we would become friends for life. I truly felt that God had brought us together for a reason. How often do you run into a person four separate times, halfway around the world, by accident? Pat was searching for something in his life, and I really prayed that he would find it. I thought that was why he came to Nepal. I was so sad to let him go, but I still had a few more weeks of my mission.

I continued working with the sisters and bonding even closer with the patients. Each new day was another opportunity to learn medicine from the sisters. The seed that was planted with that obscure pill bottle at the beginning of the trip grew rapidly until I was downright thirsty for more learning, more of the medical field. As I moved from task to task, I still stared at the medicine bottles in the dispensary, longing to know more about these *magical* pills that healed my patients.

As the days seemed to move quicker, I befriended one of the Nepali volunteers who assisted us, named Babu. He had a permanent smile that greeted me every morning with a "Namaste, Addy!"

"Namaste, Babu," I'd respond, putting my hands together and returning his welcome with a bow.

Nearly as quickly as they had arrived, the days in Nepal finally came to an end. There were tears of joy and sorrow as I left the House of Hospitality and made my way back to the states. As I disembarked, I knew without a doubt that I had been brought to Nepal for a reason. Medicine was calling my name, and I was starting to answer back.

1989

Pat's Letters

June 28, 1989

Dear Addy,

I'm sitting in a Red Robin Restaurant overlooking the shipping canal, Lake Union. A calming dusk is settling over Seattle. This is the middle of my first week back in town after more than a year in the field for a paper mill in SE Washington.

This is all quite a change. I'm leaving the casual work of blue-collar workers and construction hands for the more sterile environment of white-shirt-colored employees where folks "do lunch" and get hefty raises. I'm open to the change, though, and I look forward to what it brings.

Nepal is so far away, and yet with a mere thought, it's close again. I've thought of you often, Addy. I hope you are well. We shared a lot in such a short time, and yet there was only a little you revealed to me. That night in Chitwan, I revealed my heart and soul to you. Addy, I know you have had past hurts and losses, and often these are the reasons for wallowing in our feelings or focusing on the expressions of the here and now. It is unfortunate, but the past should only help guide the present. It shouldn't be allowed to dictate it or act as a limiting factor in our actions. After all, IT IS THE PAST! And the past is no place to live. These are just my words of wisdom to you, written with kindness and understanding.

It was so nice to feel close to someone again, especially in a faraway place. How can one night feel like it lasted for so many? I don't know if you feel the same way as I do. Do you? It was such a magical night, and the memory of it has become what gets me through my days. Time is flying by as I write this. To be continued.

October 27, 1989

Dear Addy,

This is one letter that has taken a long time to write. After two and a half months back in Seattle, I will be returning to the field at the beginning of September.

I'll start in Pasco, Washington, and carry on there until February of next year. What a life!

You will love my next story. I had lunch with a girl named Andrea. We talked about our travels. She mentioned a priest she visited in Nepal when she was a teenager. He was a seminary student teaching Sunday school. They have kept in touch since then. Twice she has visited him in Nepal. Yes, she is talking about the one and only Father Michael! The world is such a small place.

Tonight, the news has been focused on the earthquake that took place a few hours ago in your area. I sincerely hope you are safe. When I saw the videos of the collapsed interstate, I knew the early optimism expressed by some networks would soon change. I trust the Bay Area will be back on its feet soon. You and your family are in my prayers.

I've enclosed my new address as well as my home and work phone.

Please write again and tell me how things are in your life. I would love to see you and catch up on where we left off. I look forward to hearing from you and trust all is well with your sweet daughter.

With love,
Your northwest friend, Pat

I never heard from Pat again after this letter. I wrote several times, attempting to make contact, but to no avail. I tried the phone numbers he left me, and neither worked. I was concerned. *Was he okay? Why wouldn't he respond to me?*

Months later, I received a call from his sister telling me he had died in an accident at work. She said she had finally gone through all his mail and saw my name and return address on the envelopes I had sent him. She told me how he had talked to her about me many times. She apologized for not calling me sooner, but it was unnecessary. I could tell she was still recovering from his death herself. We ended the call, and I hung up the phone, sobbing into my hands.

Memories were flashing through my head. I recalled the first glimpse I had of him at the airport. I saw his beautiful smile and heard his voice offering to carry my duffel bag. I could see him sitting high on the elephant during our safari, his blond hair blowing in the wind. I watched as he took it all in, acting as if he didn't have a care in the world. I remembered how he came to my rescue as we encountered rhinos. I softly chuckled through broken cries picturing him pushing me up the tree first and then climbing up behind me. He was strong and thoughtful. Oh, how he danced around the fire to the drumbeats! He was majestic and beautiful. And now he's gone. Sitting in the chair, I softly hugged my shoulders, willing myself to feel our last embrace as he bolted out the door toward his taxi before heading back to the airport. I should have hugged him longer, squeezed him tighter. If I had known that would have been our last embrace, I would have never let him go. But I didn't know. *How could I?* I was convinced there would be many more.

How could God be so cruel? I sat there, asking Him over and over again, *why?* He brought us together! Four times, across the globe, He connected us together. *And why? Just to have it end like this? A sudden accident in a city hundreds of miles away?*

It was a long while before I recovered from Pat's passing. To this day, I still thought about him and wonder what would have happened to us if he were still alive. How might my life have been different? The heartache and pain I would have avoided.

So I wondered, which one of those overused quotes works best here? Was it the "God works in mysterious ways" or the trite old phrase "When one door closes, another opens"? What about neither? What if the best phrase for this one was "Life just happens"?

Honestly, I didn't know. But what I did know, this one really broke my heart.

November 1989–1992—back at home

Settled back at home, I returned to my employer, hoping to still have a job. Much to my surprise, I was offered a much better position in the company, a bookkeeper! The pay was higher, and the hours were a lot more normal. I was grateful for the promotion and continued with the company for the next few years. Yet through it all, I knew I wanted to do something more with medicine. I still couldn't shake the seed that was planted in Nepal. The only issue was that I had no idea what to do.

One of my friends who worked with me in bookkeeping had left the company to work at a hospital in the city. She was practicing nuclear medicine and told me before her last day, "I'm going to find a job for you there." True to her word, a few months later, she called me, and I applied for a position at the hospital.

The biggest memory I had when I first walked into the hospital was how much I loved the smell. *Really? Who loves the smell of a hospital?* Well, I did. Not sure why other than it was familiar. I felt like I had been there before.

My interview was a success, and a week later, I was offered a position as an administrative assistant in nuclear medicine—something I knew absolutely zero about. I would have to commute to the city for the job. The commute would take me roughly an hour each way. This was a brand-new experience for me, but it didn't matter. The pay was amazing. I decided to take the offer and make a massive change in my life. Nervous and pretty much clueless about what awaited me, I figured that this would place me one step closer to realizing my dream of medicine.

1992–1994

Nuclear Medicine

On my first day on the job, the person who was supposed to train me called in sick. The phone was ringing off the hook with doctors wanting their reports. One doctor was in such a hurry that he asked me to read his report out loud over the phone. I stumbled over words I had never even heard of, embarrassing myself in front of my new bosses. I felt like I did on day one of arriving in Kathmandu, only this time I was the one speaking a foreign language and still didn't have a clue as to what I was saying.

I muscled through it for him, "*Immediate post-infarction period…dipyridamole stress radionuclide myocardial perfusion imaging showing a large perfusion defect in the entire inferior and inferolateral walls more imaging needed…more often may show evidence of residual ischemia than dobutamine…*"

Finally, he cut me off with a simple, "That's fine."

The phone line went dead, and I could feel my face burning hot with a blush. This continued for another thirty minutes of phone calls until finally a doctor showed up at my desk. He was a *very* handsome Asian man. *At least I was already blushing.*

"Hi, I'm Dr. Chin," he said. "I just talked to you on the phone. Can I have a copy of that report?"

Oh no! What did I say wrong? The shade of red on my cheeks darkened even further as I clamored to explain myself. I informed him it was my first day in nuclear medicine and that I was still learning the jargon.

He was so nice. He responded sweetly, "Don't worry. I was the same way when I first started medicine."

Right! I thought. There was no way this man struggled with anything. Nevertheless, it was very kind of him to say this.

The day finally ended, and I couldn't be happier about it. After my rocky, trial-by-fire beginning, my career in nuclear medicine soared. Among the many different perks that came with working in a hospital, one of the greatest was spending time with a lot of good-looking, young resident MDs, and they all wanted to go out with the new gal. *I gladly obliged, of course.* Even the handsome Asian doctor and I got a chance to meet on occasion.

I climbed the ranks and learned as much as I possibly could until the hospital finally decided to merge, and I was laid off. Being the last person hired in the department, I was the first person to go. Lucky for me, because I was so well-liked by my supervisor, she gave me a one-month lead time before my layoff was official. She used that time to call around and arrange three interviews for me before I left! Things were looking up.

1994–1998

Medical Assistant

After leaving nuclear medicine, I ended up taking a medical assisting position with a lovely orthopedic surgeon, Dr. Lambert. Over time, he became a sort of fatherlike figure to me. Our friendship grew beyond our roles, and because of his wisdom and impact on my life, he meant the world to me. During my time with him, he taught me everything he could about orthopedic medicine. He even brought me to his surgeries to observe.

One day his colleague, Dr. Brent, couldn't assist him, so he asked me to call a PA (physician assistant) to take his place.

I asked, "What is a physician assistant?" He told me to speak with her and let her walk me through her role.

When I met her, she explained, "The short version of what I do is everything an MD does. But they provide me oversight in some form, whether that be by fax, phone, or in person."

She went on to explain the required schooling and how she had gone to Yale. She also told me that Duke had a program too. She went on to explain Duke was where the first PA program had started. *There it was again: the seed.* Suddenly a connection was made! I had found my answer: *I was going to be a PA!* I did some research, and Duke has consistently been ranked number one by US News and World Report. I thought, *Oh, this is where I want to go.*

I started researching what I needed to apply to Yale and Duke. I realized I had to go back to college and complete all the required science credits as well as other prerequisites, such as anatomy, micro-biology, physiology, chemistry, biology, statistics, and many more. The worst part was that Duke wouldn't even look at your application if you didn't have As even though they mentioned Cs as the bench-mark. This meant I would need to attend night school to ensure good grades while still managing my full-time job.

There were other requirements too, such as volunteering at least five thousand hours with the underserved population. Thankfully, I had my work with Mother Teresa, but that still wasn't enough to meet the hours. I also needed clinical experience in primary care, so I had to find another job. Because of this, I had to leave Dr. Lambert. My heart sank. He was my mentor and my friend and had become my fatherlike figure. It was hard for me to tell him that I was moving on to fulfill my dream. He took it better than I thought. Besides, we both knew we would still be friends for life. And that part has held true.

I found a full-time job in primary care and caught on to the field quickly. After one year, I was promoted to office manager, over-seeing employee scheduling, hiring, firing, paying the bills, training new medical assistants, and setting up protocols. It was quite the undertaking. It was a good job, but it wasn't what I wanted to do. I was assisting medicine, not practicing. It wouldn't be until much later that I realized how valuable this season was to me. Though my goals were elsewhere, I was still learning the vital lessons needed to run an office. I'd be thanking myself later.

Late '90s

Finishing My Sciences

I went back to school to complete the prerequisites needed to enter the physician assistant school at both Yale and Duke. I took night classes so I could keep my full-time hours. Some nights and weekends, I'd host study groups at my house. I made it my goal to be an outstanding student, and I poured my heart and soul into my learning. It was during orientation at Duke that I learned to immediately put aside any applicants who didn't maintain a 4.0 GPA in their sciences (even though they said differently on their website). This was their easy way to weed out applicants since so many applied. There were only fifty students selected at a time for each class.

As I progressed in school, I found a tribe of like-minded students who shared my same passion and drive. Their names were Mae and Ann. This would start a lifetime of friendship that still thrived even decades later. When we had the same classes together, we were basically tied at the hip—day and night. This excluded, of course, the handsome Bulgarian student who helped me with my chemistry. Dean was very smart, and it didn't hurt that he had an accent. It was my thing after all. I also loved a man with a good brain as well.

He made chemistry look easy. There was only one problem; he'd often get distracted by me. His famous line as we studied was, "We could make such good chemistry together!" When I finally found out his age, I nearly died. He had seemed so mature to me, but he was barely twenty-three, and I was already thirty-eight! I knew my daughter would die if she even guessed at me thinking of being with somebody this age. So I forced myself to focus on his brain, not his body.

Then there was my study partner, Bret. He was my study partner for anatomy, of all things. Bret was a hot fireman (pun intended) who was studying for paramedic school. He had also recently been separated from his wife. *What was it about a man in uniform that was so attractive?* He would walk into the anatomy lab in his uniform, and I'd melt. Perhaps it was the fact that my former husband was also a firefighter that made me so *aware of the occupation.*

Sitting with Bret brought back memories of my earlier years in the dating pool before marriage. I made it a point to date a different firefighter on every shift, making sure they never met.

There was Brad on the morning shift. He was a bodybuilder who would take me for early Sunday morning rides on his motorcycle. We'd trace the beach coastline, stopping to have breakfast and then returning. My dad approved of Brad because of the motorcycle.

Then there was Ryan on the evening shift. He was cute and funny enough to make me laugh.

But I'll never forget the one who stole my heart, *Marc, on the midnight shift.* This one I ended up marrying. He became the father to my daughter, Nicole. To this day, we have stayed good friends despite the divorce. We are such good friends, in fact, that I was able to fix him up on a date with his next wife. Yes, firefighters had their way with my heart, and like a moth to the flame, I couldn't seem to help myself with their charm.

But I knew I shouldn't play with fire here. There was too much on the line. Bret was good-looking, yes, but I needed to stay focused. It didn't stop the heart flutters, though. I could still see his steamy steel-blue eyes as he looked at me over the anatomy textbooks and that smile he had that seemed to relax even the most intimate parts of me. He had a wonderful sense of humor that made me laugh so hard at times that I thought I would wet my pants! I couldn't help but still wonder where he is today and how those soft blue eyes are doing.

Unfortunately, my attractions weren't reserved solely for fellow classmates. My biology teacher, Will, was the primary target of all young women on the campus. I didn't know a single girl who didn't want to date him. He was an absolute bombshell. One of those that would make you drop random adjectives under your breath as he walked by you in the hall, like *"He's gorgeous"* or *"So hot."* He was tall, lean, had piercing brown eyes, dark, wavy brown hair, brilliant, of course, and hilarious. Until I met him, I had never thought of biology as a particularly fun subject, but he had the ability to make it both engaging and entertaining. I remember our discussion on photosynthesis; he dressed like a plant to teach the lecture. And when we were studying muscles, he dressed like Superman. With every new subject, there was always some type of costume to go along with it.

At one point, Will approached me concerning my grades. "Addy, why are you getting Bs? Don't you have a study group?"

I replied, "Yes, I do! We get together every weekend."

He said, "Then I don't understand. You should be getting As. Would you and your group like to come to my house this weekend so I can observe how you are studying? I could try and give you some tips."

I thought my knees were going to give out. The heartthrob professor at my school was asking *my study group* to *his house*! As I suspected, the girls were ecstatic when I told them.

Will gave me the gate code to get back to his place. We couldn't believe it when we got to his house. As soon as we arrived, he gave us a tour. This wasn't any old house. It was a full farm with ninety undomesticated animals. There was one house devoted to reptiles, several types of iguanas, and all different species of snakes, including a massive boa constrictor that was inside his own cage. On the farm itself, there were plenty of chickens, pigs, and llamas. An adorable white cockatiel named Ginger stayed inside the main house with Will. I couldn't believe it; this man truly was a *biology teacher.*

He lived and breathed what he taught.

For many weekends, we studied at his place. He helped tremendously, and I felt compelled to somehow repay him, so I asked him. He said it would be helpful if I would be willing to take care of the farm when he went away on some weekends and vacations. *Um…yes!* He said he would be willing to pay me, but I refused. Still, he insisted and paid me a very generous amount! I was a single mother, so it was much appreciated.

The girls were convinced he had a crush on me because he always wanted to help me. He never made a pass at me, though, and was very professional in all our meetings, so I didn't get that vibe. One night when I was at his house training how to feed all the animals, I saw a petite Asian girl cooking in his kitchen. Later, I came to realize that she had been with Will on his weekend getaways.

Will and I slowly became close friends. We even began confiding in each other about our relationships and love interests. When he started considering ending things with the sweet Thai girl, Achara (we called her Angel, which was the translation for the name because no one could pronounce her real one), Will informed me he had his eye on another gal. This made sense as there was a line of women waiting for him. Over time, he started coming to my house for dinner, and my mom even started babysitting his bird, Ginger, when he was out of town. It got to the point where he even started bringing women over for our approval! These poor women. *If they only knew!* He would tell them I was his adopted sister and my mom was his adopted mother.

We would go for hikes together often. He knew all the names of the wildflowers and the scat (poop) from all the animals. When the moon was full, we would hike one of the mountains near his home to one of the outlooks of the valley. He would call the owls, and they would call back to him. It was magical. This was Will's specialty. He had even completed his doctoral thesis on *one hundred bird calls.* Later he told me he regretted that as it was probably the most difficult undertaking of his life. He'd often take me bird-watching. For my birthday one year, he bought me binoculars and a bird-watching book to help me identify the different types. When he would take his marine biology classes to some weekend outings at beach, I'd tag along when I could. I was in awe of his knowledge. He knew so many different species along the ocean shore. He was such a brilliant man, and I felt honored that he shared so much with me.

At one point, while Will was in Alaska, I was tending the farm for him. He called me to check in and asked a question I had never heard before.

"Has the boa constrictor had a bowel movement yet?"

"What do you mean by bowel movement?" I asked nervously.

"Look inside the cage. Let me know if you see any poop. If you don't, call Drew and Pete to come up there. You will need help massaging the snake to help it have a BM. They know how to help you."

Um, excuse me? I was shaken. "Will, is this some kind of joke? I know how you like to joke."

With a serious tone, he responded, "No, Addy, this is serious."

I replied with a small "Okay…" and hung up the phone. My hands were trembling.

Understand this: *I am deathly afraid of snakes.* This fear started as a child when my brother would find harmless garter snakes in the grass and throw them at me. He'd even dangle them on the clothesline outside while I was hanging clothes to dry. *So snakes weren't really my thing.*

But Will was serious, and I had agreed to watch the farm. So I had to do the deed. Drew, Pete, and I stood in a circle holding this twelve-foot boa between us and massaged its body. It was hot, and I was sweating. The snake liked my warmth so much that it wanted to stay by me. *This was…great.* Throughout the process, there were moments where I thought, *You couldn't pay me enough money to ever do this again.* After thirty minutes, we put the snake back in the cage and prayed earnestly that we'd find a bowel movement the next day. Lucky for me, it was waiting on me when I returned. I prayed to God and to Will that I would never have to do anything like that again!

I had a blast with Will, and even better, I ended up getting an A in his class.

While in college, I decided I would do anything and everything to make my application stand out from everyone else. I became a Eucharistic minister and a detention minister, where I would go to the local county jail and nearby central prison. I even started working at a free clinic downtown on my days off. I worked extremely hard to maintain a 4.0 grade point average and volunteered for everything I could possibly fit into my already busy schedule. I joined the Alpha Gamma Sigma Honor Society, where I eventually became chapter vice president and joined the local environmental society.

It wasn't long before I started receiving recognition for my hard work. I was so pleased when the dean of the college informed me I was to be honored at the state capitol in Raleigh by the governor for getting first place in *the All-California Academic Team* and landing nominee for the *All-USA Academic Team*. My family attended the ceremony as well. It was an honor. I received other awards as well, including the *Honor Society Special Achievement Award 1996, Outstanding Service Award 1997, Blue Chip Fundraising Award 1997, Excellence Service Award 1997, Outstanding Service Award 1998*, and the *ASCOM 1998 Leadership Award*.

Everything I did was focused on being selected by the best schools possible. I wanted to stand out among my peers, and stand out I did. It took me four years of night school to complete all the courses required for admission into the graduate program.

As our commencement ceremony approached, I was excited to learn from my speech professor that I had been selected to deliver the speech. *Me? Wow! What an honor!*

When the day came to give my speech, I looked out at my classmates, professors, and my family, who had helped throughout the first leg of this long journey in which I was traveling. I paused for a brief moment, taking it all in. I knew I would never have another moment like this. I scanned the audience, looking at the familiar faces until I found Will among my professors. He winked at me and gave me a thumbs-up. I smiled, took a deep breath, and began my commencement speech as a small tear rolled down my face. This was a special moment in my life, one that I often still thought of with tears in my eyes. I made sure my speech had laughter, joy, some tears, but ended with triumph and words of encouragement for my classmates. The class, professors, and families gave a big round of applause at the end of my speech, and I was beaming.

When it was over, I managed to graduate with top honors. My father was an old-school individual who didn't believe women should attend college. He had only ever approved of my brother going. As I walked across the aisle and received my diploma, I thought of all the sacrifices I had made and the obstacles I had overcome. It meant the world to me. And it meant even more knowing he was watching me do it. But it was over, and now I was ready to apply to Duke and Yale.

The Late 1990s

Busy Dreams and Office Romances

I continued working my job in primary care, anxiously awaiting interviews for the programs. To my surprise and excitement, I was scheduled for both! The interviews were oral and written. I was nervous, but this was what I wanted, and I felt confident. I left the interviews with a sense of pride and assurance.

Within a month of completing the interviews, I received letters in the mail from both universities. Unfortunately, Duke denied my application. On the other hand, Yale informed me I was number one on the waitlist! Number one? *That's great!* I was assured that somebody would surely drop out, so I shouldn't be worried. I couldn't shake a feeling of disappointment, however. I was hoping I would get to choose between both. But I felt lucky to get into at least one knowing how competitive they were.

Time went on, and I realized no one was dropping out. I didn't get into Yale either. Now I had to wait another year to apply again.

This was another good spot to consider those God questions. *Was He working in those mysterious ways again? Was this happening for a reason, and was He testing my patience?* Once again, I really didn't know. All I knew was I was extremely disappointed.

I decided to pick myself back up and carry on, believing that there *was* some reason unknown to me. *Maybe there was something else I needed to do before moving on.* I continued my work in primary care, still absorbing everything in medicine while waiting to apply again. I also applied to the nursing program in addition to PA school, just in case. This way, if it didn't work out in the end, I could go the nurse practitioner route. I refused to sit idly by and let the door into medicine slam in my face. *Not this time.*

One day my boss at the time, Dr. Ellis, informed me he was bringing in a new MD to help him out. It was my job to *show him the ropes* of the office. Dr. Ellis had known Dr. Matthew Alden when he was a resident and thought he was brilliant. We definitely could use the help.

When Dr. Alden arrived later that day, all the girls at the front office were giddy. I asked one of them what was happening.

They closed the glass window in the office that separated us from the waiting area. "Wait until you lay eyes on this new doc, Addy. He is so handsome."

I cracked the window open and saw an extremely handsome man sitting in the waiting room chair, and my heart melted. I closed the glass window and turned toward the girls.

With a sinister smile, I whispered, "Hands off, ladies. He's mine."

One of them laughed and playfully complained, "But you *just* said you were done with men for the next year!"

I had recently broken up with a boyfriend when I made this statement. "Well, I've changed my mind."

Matthew was a cross between Brad Pitt and a younger Robert Redford. He was mesmerizing, and with a doctor's title next to his name, well…it was a *prize package.*

I brought him back to my office, introducing myself as the office manager. I explained that I would be working *directly* with him throughout the next few months, showing him the ins and outs of our office procedures, hours, schedules, etc.

We spent many hours together going through office protocols. One day in passing, I mentioned to him I had applied to PA school. He seemed intrigued. I told him there were a few holes in my application, such as I didn't know how to read an EKG or perform a *history* on a patient. He quickly offered to help me…*after-hours.* Thus began the next chapter of my life.

For many evenings after work, we took our time going over EKGs and medical histories. It became quite clear to both of us that we had feelings for each other. Quickly, we developed a friendship through sharing stories of our families. Christmas was approaching, and I asked what he was doing for the holiday. He informed me he'd be spending it by himself because his family wasn't nearby. I felt bad for him. No one should have to spend Christmas alone. I invited him to join my family. I was shocked I did this and even more shocked that he accepted! My family was also surprised that I would invite a complete stranger to Christmas dinner. But once he arrived, he was quickly accepted.

My daughter was intrigued by his intelligence and quickly asked if he would assist her with chemistry. He happily agreed. That night, after everyone left, we told each other goodbye on the front porch.

He whispered, "You know, I can't get involved with someone I work with. It's unethical. I know we have this attraction to each other, but there is nothing we can do about it."

I didn't let that stop me. Quickly I replied, "Well, I'm going to get into PA school this time. I just know it. When that happens, I won't be an employee much longer. Then it won't be a problem."

With that answer, he lowered his head and kissed me. A magical, crazy, tumultuous love story began.

Matthew kept his promise to Nicole and helped her with her chemistry. She was in awe of how he would run his fingers over the pages of the textbook, turning them one by one, only to then stop and explain to her what everything meant. He had a way of simplifying it all to where she fully understood it.

We had many lunches and dinners together and shared our life stories. I learned that he had moved back to Utah, his home state, to build a practice. He didn't like it there and decided to return to North Carolina, where he had completed his residency. I could sense there was something more to the story, but he didn't tell me. One night while we were sitting on the couch, I noticed his shoes were worn, with holes in the soles. I thought, *How could a doctor have holes in his shoes?* It was odd, but I let it pass.

Many times, he'd fly to New York. He'd tell me it was for business and that he was trying to raise money for a new venture.

He only did this when he wasn't working for Dr. Ellis. When he would call me from New York, our conversations were cut off early because he always had a business dinner to go to. The behavior was somewhat strange, but I was head over heels for this man, so to me, it was just a new person with new habits.

1999

Back to Nepal

When the time finally came, I completed my second application for Duke as well as Yale and for the nursing program.

Once again, I was given another interview by both universities. An interview was unnecessary for the nursing program. It was just an application and then admission if you met the requirements. When I attended the Duke interview, the interviewer mentioned that I had applied before for the program.

"What made you apply again?"

I responded, "I'm going to keep applying until you accept me. Even if I need to attend in a wheelchair by the time you do. I'm determined to get into this program one way or the other."

She laughed. It was funny, sure, but I was deadly serious.

Back at the office, I mentioned to Dr. Simons, a doctor that worked for Dr. Ellis, about my experience in Nepal. She was very interested and asked if I might consider returning and volunteering again at a higher level.

"Do you still have a contact there?" she wondered.

Father Michael and I had remained friends and stayed in contact. We began brainstorming how we could revisit. Soon word spread around our office, and we started to see who might want to go with us.

I contacted Father Michael and asked what the current needs were.

"Dentistry, something for dysentery, and sunglasses," was his answer.

Sunglasses? Apparently, because the sun was so bright there, people developed cataracts quite early due to a lack of protection for their eyes. When I asked where the need was the greatest, he told me about a little village called Tumlingtar and Pokara. He offered to connect us with the right parties and get the trip set up. We were willing to commit to three full weeks, one per village. The other week was reserved for travel time and visitations. I wanted to go back to Pashupatinath, where it all began for me.

Dr. Simons and I put together a team of two dentists, another medical assistant like myself, and a nutritionist. We also worked with an ophthalmologist who donated two hundred pairs of sunglasses. We gathered as many antibiotics as we could for dysentery and made the final preparations to leave. I was ecstatic. I couldn't believe that ten years later, I would be going back to Nepal. My life had come full circle.

Once again, I bid goodbye to my family. This time Nicole was almost sixteen, so she wasn't as sad to see her mother leave for three weeks! My romance with Dr. Alden had bloomed, so it was much harder to say goodbye to him. This was in 1999, so contact was difficult, especially across the world.

We flew into Kathmandu and quickly transferred to a small plane that would take us to our first stop, Tumlingtar. Landing on a grassy runway, we could see the whole village at the end of it, ready to greet us. They were all bowing to us with their hands clasped in prayer, offering us excited namastes. Our contacts brought us to our accommodations and showed us where our clinic would be for the next seven days. The food? Take one guess: *dal bhat for a week!*

The next day, we started bright and early at 7:00 a.m. When we arrived at the clinic, the Nepali people were already lined up outside. We worked twelve hours per day. We were each provided with a translator to carry out our duties with our patients. I mainly saw patients with dysentery, providing them with the appropriate medication. If they were more complicated, I would triage them to Dr. Simons. I felt like a hamster on a wheel. The same routine over and over again for an entire week. When we wrapped on the seventh day, we said our goodbyes to the lovely people of Tumlingtar and headed to Pokhara.

Luckily, we didn't have to land on grass this time. Pokhara was much more developed than Tumlingtar. That didn't stop them from serving us dal bhat again every day! Our routine was basically the same as in Tumlingtar. The Nepali people all needed the same type of care. The days were just as long, and the people were equally as thankful. At the end of the week, we said goodbye, hugged, and waved to the good people of Pokhara and headed toward Kathmandu to meet up with Father Michael.

For the first time in ten years, I could stay at the House of Hospitality again. Father Michael was exactly as I remembered him, with that infectious smile that spread ear to ear. He welcomed us all into the house. After we settled, we all shared our experiences in the two villages, and that night held a big party.

Later that evening, the phone rang, and Father Michael told me it was my mother. I was worried something was wrong. Taking the phone, my heart was beating fast. *Please don't be bad news*, I thought.

"Mom?" There was a delay on the phone line. "Is everything okay?"

"Addy," she began. "I have two envelopes here. One from Yale and one from Duke. Do you want me to open them?"

"Yes!"

The sound of paper being torn on the other end sent a shiver down my spine.

"Okay, I'm opening the Yale one first," she said as if she was a host on a game show. The line went silent.

"Mom? I can't hear you."

Suddenly, her voice came through broken, but it wasn't the reception. I could hear excitement billowing from her words, "'Dear Ms. DeLucca…this letter is to inform you that you have been selected for the incoming physician assistant class of 2000 at Yale School of Physician Assistant. Please let us know within the next two weeks of your acceptance…"

I nearly dropped the phone and started screaming.

Father Michael leaned toward me, concerned. "Is everything okay, Addy?"

I said, "Yes, I have been accepted to Yale PA School!"

"Oh, God has answered your prayers, Addy!"

My mom started yelling on the phone line as I put her back to my ear. "Wait! I still need to open Duke!"

Once again, the sound of rustling paper.

"Dear Ms. DeLucca…this letter is to inform you that you have been selected for the incoming Duke Physician Assistant School of Medicine class of 2000. Please let us know within the next two weeks of your acceptance…"

The phone dropped in my hand, and I started screaming again. Father Michael came running back again. All the others were in tow.

"What happened?" he said.

"I got into Duke too!"

Dr. Simons was jumping up and down with joy. She was a Duke graduate, so of course, she was partial to the school. "Oh, you have to go there!"

My poor mom was trying to be heard above the noise. "Addy, are you there?"

I laughed and picked the phone back up. "Yes, so sorry, Mom! I was just telling everyone the news."

"What are you going to do?" she asked.

"I don't know! I can't decide right now. I'm just happy to get into PA school!"

We continued to celebrate that night as the culmination of ten years of journeying unfolded before my eyes. Here I stood in the same house that a decade ago birthed in me the desire to pursue medicine. And now after everything, I had what I needed to take the next step forward. Lying in bed that night, I thanked God for bringing me back to Nepal, where it all started. The next day, I told Father Michael I wanted to go to Pashupatinath tomorrow to see how much it had changed. He told me he would take me there before we left for the airport.

On the final day in Nepal, we got up early and had breakfast. We packed our things and, on the way to the airport, stopped by

Pashupatinath. I got out of the car and walked toward the opening of the hallway. I heard a voice call out, "Addy!" I turned around, and there was Babu. I couldn't believe my eyes. Ten years later and he was still there taking care of the place. *And above all else, he remembered me!* Instead of the typical *namaste*, we embraced each other. Father Michael translated to him that we had set up health-care clinics in Tumlingtar and Pokhara. He was smiling from ear to ear and kept repeating "Dhanyabaad" ("Thank you" in Nepali). Father Michael shared the good news about me going into medicine.

"It's because of what she learned here," he told him in Nepalese.

Babu's eyes widened, and he hugged me again. I said my good-byes to him and to Pashupatinath and once again thanked God and the Missionaries of Charity for leading me to my passion. I'd never forget Nepal, Father Al for his belief in me, the psychic who steered me in the beginning, and of course, Father Michael, who made it all possible.

The long flights, airport exchanges, and car rides toward the house were a blur. I couldn't wait to get home and share the news with Matthew. *What is he going to think? Who knows, maybe we will be starting a new chapter too!*

I knew I had to decide and fast. Everyone thought I was crazy to even consider not going to Duke. They told me that just having the school's name on my résumé would open up any door I wanted.

"But I do like the curriculum at Yale," I would respond.

To make matters more complicated, I did receive word that I was accepted into the nursing program as well. It's funny how life worked. A year earlier, nothing. *Now suddenly, I have to make a decision between all three. I guess God can be mysterious, huh?*

After my own considerations and with the help of all the influence from Dr. Simons, my friends, family, and of course, Matthew, I finally made my decision. I was going to Duke.

Matthew approached me shortly after the decisions were made and said, "I really want to help you through this program. I thought that maybe I could move in with you. After all, you're going to have to learn in twenty-four months what has taken me four years."

Wow, I was in shock. I was both confused and overwhelmed. He hadn't even said the *L* word yet. I could tell he really cared for me, and this offer melted my heart. It *would* be nice to have his brain close by while I worked my way through the program too. I knew it was going to be extremely difficult. He even offered to help me financially, which was quite generous.

"I have a lot of business ventures that are about to pay off," he informed me.

This must have been related to the trips to New York. He tried to explain to me what they were, but I couldn't understand what he was saying. It had something to do with prototypes that could change health care. I wasn't sure how that was incorporated with medicine, but I took him at his word.

We decided to get a two-bedroom apartment between Duke University and Matthew's job. We agreed that I could use one room for studying and have an extra bed in case Nicole ever wanted to spend the night. I would take the train to Duke, and he would take my car to his job, and he would pick me up at the train station after classes. For some reason, Matthew didn't have a vehicle.

When I questioned him on this, he responded with, "Oh, I really never needed one."

"Okay, but what did you use to drive to my house?"

"That was my roommate's car," he explained. This confused me.

"Your roommate? I didn't even know you had a roommate."

He stumbled a tad with his response. "I had just moved back to the area. It was just until I got back on my feet."

I had often wondered why he only invited me to his place one time. His roommate must have been out of town. It was only a one-bedroom apartment, so he must have been sleeping on the couch. *Poor guy! He was too embarrassed to tell me.*

As time went on, he began to tell me more about how he had his own business right after completing his residency and was doing quite well. He started the teaching program at a local hospital for struggling students, and it really took off. Basically, it was a tutoring program because he was so good at teaching.

"I could walk into Saks Fifth Avenue and buy anything I wanted," he would tell me. "Handmade suits in multiple colors, shoes made from the finest leather—cost was never an issue."

So what happened? Well, like all things that were successful, others saw it and wanted it. He told me how it had been taken from him and that he was still trying to prove it was his. In doing so, he nearly went broke. That was why he decided to move back to Utah and live with his family. He was looking to recoup what he'd lost and try to rebuild his life, but he missed North Carolina too much and decided to move back. When he got the call from Dr. Ellis to work for him, he knew it was his opportunity to start over again.

I was so relieved when he told me all this. Suddenly, I felt better about the holes in his shoes and the couch surfing with his roommate. It all made so much more sense now.

2000

LOVE AND OTHER DRUGS
IN BARCELONA, SPAIN

Right before school began, Matthew and I decided to take a trip to Barcelona, Spain. This was my last chance to travel for a long time, and we both loved the city for its beauty and culture. We told Nicole she could invite one of her friends and go with us. Matthew and I planned to spend a few days just the two of us before the girls arrived.

It was going to be such a great trip for the four of us. Our plan was to stay two weeks in the country. Nicole decided to bring her best friend, Tina. Matthew offered to pay for half of the trip, but to keep things simple, we agreed to put all charges on my personal credit card. He would reimburse me directly for his half.

Matthew and I arrived in Barcelona and rented a car for our drive to country. There, our villa awaited us. I was so excited. It all sounded so romantic! I was glad Matthew was driving because the *autostrada* was nerve-racking! The cars buzzed by us so fast it seemed like they were going at least one hundred miles per hour. *Who knows, maybe they were!*

The villa we rented was built in the 1870s and sat atop a hill overlooking vineyards as well as olive and fruit trees. It was a magnificent view of the valley. My favorite was overlooking the bright yellow sunflowers down the hill. It looked as if Van Gogh had stopped on his way to Spain, laid down a canvas, and painted a field of bright yellow and green. The property was roughly seven acres, and the surrounding garden offered complete privacy. Our suite had a large, picturesque window with shutters that opened onto that same breathtaking field of sunflowers. Our four-poster mahogany bed was positioned perfectly in front of the window so we could bask in the view.

We unpacked our luggage, and Matthew mentioned he wanted to take a nap.

"Well, I want to get this airplane travel smell off me," I responded. "I'm going to take a shower."

As I turned to walk toward the shower, Matthew grabbed my hand tenderly and pulled me back toward him. His lips began lightly brushing over my neck and shoulder as his fingertips traced down my arms and met my fingertips. After a quick squeeze, they started the journey back up arms. Thudding shock waves pulsed through me as I felt myself give in more and more.

My head fell to the side as I allowed him further access to the warm skin of my neck. He softly laid his hands on my stomach and began massaging me in such a way that I felt myself gasp. I noticed my lips were quivering. His massaging continued up and down my arms, legs, and belly. I felt myself relax, my back arch, and my arms tingle. I sighed deeply as he began to slide his hands down to my waist.

He pushed me slowly against the wall with my shoulders and seat resting on the ancient plaster. I pushed myself gently backward, deeper into the wall as I began biting my lip, anticipating. I wanted so desperately for him to kiss me. As if on cue, he leaned closer, nearly touching my lips. I could feel his breath against my skin. My legs were trembling. Then he ignored my lips, kissing my cheek. His lips made their way to my neck, then my shoulders.

I was so hot. I could feel my heart beating against his chest. Its rhythm began matching his own. They were both beating faster. Every time my mouth would come close to his, he'd back away. *He was denying me.*

It was both frustrating and incredibly sexy. *He surprises me.* With a rhythmic motion, he put his hands between my legs, pulling up my dress. He didn't do anything except hold his hot hand still above my panties. He was steady. I gasped quickly. Suddenly I felt safe and warm all over.

He reached his other hand behind my head, grabbed a fistful of my hair, and firmly pulled my head back. It wasn't painful, just demanding. Finally, his lips touched mine. Once again, simply frozen…still. It was as if we both were attempting to absorb all the energy of that moment before proceeding.

We broke for a quick moment and stared into each other's eyes. I had had enough of the denial. With a forceful motion, I grabbed him by the neck and started kissing him passionately. My hand found its way down his body and began rubbing the outline of his member through his pants.

For what seemed like an eternity, we kissed in deep passion. The room temperature began to lift higher and higher. *Or is that just me?* My senses began to mix into a swirling concoction of pleasure as I felt my whole composure begin to lose control. Pleasure began to reach a boiling point as he rubbed in circular motions through my underwear, slowly and firmly. He continued to tease me with little kisses. Sometimes on my lips, sometimes on my neck. When he nibbled on my ear, I felt breath in my ear. Sexual desire rose quickly and fiercely as heat spread throughout my body.

With another swift motion, he turned his body and began pushing me toward the bed. When my legs reached the edge, I fell backward, vulnerable. His hands began to search down my legs, starting at my hips and continuing up and down. He explored every inch from my ankles to my thighs, to my… *Oh boy.*

Through closed eyes, I heard him unbuckle his pants and the sound of his trousers falling to the floor. Softly, he lay on top of me. I could feel his hardness through his underwear as it pressed deliberately into my midsection. He stood back up briefly and pulled my underwear down from my hips past my feet. Then he assumed his position again, holding himself slightly up with his strong arms outlining my shoulders against the bed. With his face, he started rubbing my breasts, placing my nipples in his mouth, and sucking them as hard as I would let him. *And I let him…hard.*

I began to moan softly, and he lowered his head between my legs and kissed me in ways I hadn't thought were possible. The pleasure was overwhelming. He stopped only long enough to look up and wink in my direction before plunging back down toward my waist. By now I was moaning very loudly. In between breaths, he started to command that I tell him I wanted more. I happily obliged and began to repeat how much more I wanted from him. Finally, after what seemed like an eternity of pleasure, I finally screamed his name out loud, feeling as if I was going to pass out.

"I want you inside of me!" I yelled breathily.

When he raised his body, I realized how hard he was. I was surprised he wasn't about to burst at that very moment.

I reached toward him and began rubbing his member softly as he whispered in my ear, "Just think how this will feel inside of you. But don't be so impatient." He then leaned closer and added, "You can't have me yet."

He then grabbed me and placed my hands behind my back. He then turned me over onto my stomach and smacked me on the backside. It stung, but it felt so good. I winced in pain and pleasure. He turned me back over and slid himself inside me. I felt the firmness of his manhood pushing deep inside me, invading me. My legs started to tremble. I felt my knees buckle briefly while he pushed all the way in. Then he began to move back and forth. I could feel my hips pushing against his in a rhythm that nearly intoxicated me. I felt completely full when he suddenly stopped.

"Just wait," he whispered. "I'm letting you relax. Letting you enjoy the feeling of me inside you."

Then the rhythmic movement started to pick back up, speeding fast until we were galloping together in the sheets. I started moaning louder and biting my lip. I tried to turn my head around to look at him in the mirror across the room. I wanted to see our bodies entwined. At that moment, I felt like we were one. I felt sexy for the first time in my life. He grabbed both my arms and folded them behind my back. By now he was pounding harder than ever. I couldn't think of anything else at that moment. I was utterly lost in a sea of pleasure. All I managed to do was scream his name over and over.

We both fell asleep for a few hours afterward. When I woke up, I decided to finally take that shower. I slipped quietly out of bed and tiptoed into the bathroom. I let the warm water run over my body and through my hair. It felt so good. The Italian soap smelled like honey. I lathered my whole body to try and get rid of the travel smell. I heard the shower door creek open; I didn't turn around because I knew it had to be Matthew. His body pressed against mine. The warm water soaked us as he grabbed the soap and lathered it on both of us. His hands were circling around my breasts, slowly stopping every once in and while to pinch my nipples. He started caressing my neck with his lips and slowly sucking at the nap of my neck. I could feel the fire between my thighs start back up. His hands started running up and down my legs, slowly teasing the inside of my groin.

I would try to turn around, but he would stop me, whispering in a soft, seductive breath, "Take it slow." Then he would start the routine all over again with my breasts, neck, and legs and finally put his hand between my thighs, whispering in my ear, "Does it feel good?"

All I could do was moan. My breath would catch at every light touch, taking in the sweet scent of the honey soap. He reached to move my drenched hair of curls, pushing it over one of my shoulders, so he could continue nipping and sucking at the other side of my neck. He finally turned off the water and gathered me in his arms and carried me to the bed.

We lay there for a moment as he looked into my eyes and said, "Addy, I'm falling in love with you. I know it has only been a few months, but I have never felt this way about anyone."

I smiled and said, "Me too, Matthew."

I felt like this man had cast a love spell over me. I was completely taken with him and couldn't think of anywhere else I would rather be than at that villa at that very moment. With renewed energy, he climbed on top of me and started passionately kissing me. I could feel the firmness of his manhood between my legs. He moved down and nibbled at my neck, slowly moving to my breasts, and began caressing one while sucking on the other. I could hardly contain myself. I wanted him so badly *again!* I had never been so aroused and wet. He licked my navel as he continued to travel down my body toward my thighs. I didn't think I could handle any more arousal. His mouth moved toward my burning midsection. His hand reached toward my lips as he opened me. His tongue touched my inner parts.

"Stop! I want this to last!" I managed to yell.

He rolled onto his back as I climbed on top of him. We kissed passionately for a long time. I began sucking at the nape of his neck and his earlobe and working my way down to his nipples, teasing them gently with my teeth. I heard him moan. I ran my tongue down to his navel and in between his loins. I began teasing him with my tongue while running my hands up and down his muscular legs and over his abs. I pulled his legs apart and took him into my mouth slowly while I watched his face. I teased his nipples with my fingers and ran my tongue around the tip of his shaft, slowly taking him in and out of my mouth. He moaned louder. Slowly, I crawled on top of him, letting the hardness of his shaft enter the burning fire between my legs. I loved controlling the pace. I was able to catch my breath with each movement. I would go between thrusting to him, clutching my hips and rear end while gently pulling me forward and pushing me back. This went on for what felt like an eternity as we took turns. Finally, we were both so exhausted we fell asleep, only to wake up and do it all over again and again.

In between all this lovemaking, we talked about life and what we wanted in our future.

I asked him, "Have you never been married?"

"I've been engaged two times."

"What!" I was shocked.

Matthew continued, "Well, would you rather me be telling you I was married two times and divorced two times?" He smiled innocently. "They just weren't meant to be."

Matthew was forty years old. He was your typical bachelor that everyone still wanted. Aging had made him even more handsome. A good-looking doctor that everyone wanted to marry. Dr. Ellis had told me when Matthew was a resident in training, he had all the nurses after him. Apparently, he dated a different nurse on every shift, but none of them knew about the other one. *Hmm, that sounded familiar.*

Matthew asked, "Would you ever consider having any more children?"

"Well, I always wanted one more, but the opportunity has never presented itself."

Matthew responded, "Well, don't freak out, but I can picture myself having a child with you."

I was taken aback by this comment. My head was spinning. This relationship was moving so fast. A part of me was excited and flattered, while another was scared. Scared because I was typically a methodical person who planned everything out. This began to fall outside of my comfort zone. *But maybe that was a good thing.*

I smiled and said, "I would love that…in time." I was falling for this man, hard and fast.

The days grew closer before the girls would arrive. Matthew and I began to grow closer as well. We went for walks in the vineyards and had romantic dinners at night. We had deeper, more complex talks about our past and our future. It became clearer to me that he wanted to build a future that involved Nicole and me.

Time seemed to move by slowly, and I soaked up every minute I could between intimate moments with Matthew and the scenery of Barcelona. Matthew never left my side except for quick trips to the bathroom and momentary escapes to retrieve something he had brought with him from his toiletry bag. I could never quite figure out what it was until one night, I watched him go back for it. Taking a quick glimpse, I recognized the familiar shape and color of a pill bottle. It was clear by looking at it that the contents were narcotic in nature. I hadn't heard anything about pain or problems from Matthew, so naturally, this came as a shock. I found out after a short inquiry that he took the pills because of chronic headaches. Something inside me felt this was odd, but the sheer joy of my surroundings quickly pushed the thought down deep and hid it away.

When Nicole and Tina arrived, we became tourists. We visited the wineries, learned about olive oil, and went out for fabulous dinners. We toured Montserra, medieval Girona, and Figueres's Salvador Dali Museum. We indulged in delicious tapas, paella, sangria. We even managed to take in a Flamenco show. The girls were having the time of their life. All was well until suddenly, Matthew said he had to fly home. It was urgent for one of his business ventures…in New York he said.

"What?" I asked. "We still have four days left of our trip!"

Matthew had also been doing all the driving at this point, and I was scared to death driving on the roads in Barcelona. I was extremely upset with him and couldn't understand why. He insisted it was so urgent and had to leave the next day.

We all drove Matthew to the airport. The girls and I decided to stay in town to visit more sites. The part I didn't tell the girls was that Matthew had never reimbursed me for the trip. I wasn't sure if he planned to do that when we returned, but now he had basically left me with no money, and my credit card was nearly maxed out because of the trip.

The girls sometimes complained, wishing Matthew were still there because "at least we could spend money!" They'd add, "He wasn't as cheap as you are!"

I felt so bad, but I didn't want to burst their bubble about Matthew. I knew Nicole really liked him. This was the first man I had brought home that she really liked in a long, long time. On the way back to our villa, it was pouring rain, and I'd never been so afraid to drive in my life. Cars were whizzing by me as if I was standing still. These Spanish were crazy drivers. We made it through Barcelona finally and came back home. Matthew had been placed on a pedestal, and I was definitely not the fun one in the girls' eyes.

When I got home, I was exhausted. I knew that I only had one day to recover before I had to go back to work. I was nearly done working for Dr. Ellis before starting school at Duke. Matthew was still flying to New York for his meetings and then would fly directly into Raleigh, North Carolina, where he'd take a taxi to the office.

That night, I tried calling his cell phone, but it went to voice mail. I remembered where he said he was staying, so I called his hotel room to check in with him and see how everything was going with his business venture. I asked for Matthew Alden's room, and the receptionist forwarded me. A woman answered the phone on the other end. At first, I thought they had given me the wrong room.

"Is this Matthew Alden's room?"

"Yes," the voice answered.

I said, "Who is this?"

"This is Stephannie, his girlfriend."

My face went red. "Well, that's impossible because I am his girlfriend!" I felt compelled to fight for my integrity and defend my position as "his" girlfriend.

I explained to her that we had just spent almost two weeks in Spain together. I said we rented an apartment in North Carolina, near Duke, so that he could help with physician assistant school at Duke and that we had been dating for the last three months. I told her we had even talked about our future together and having a child together. She went on to tell me that they had met in Utah over a year ago and that she had just moved to New York to visit him. She informed me that they had been dating for more than a year. She was smart enough to realize that we had both been fooled by him. She wasn't mad at me at all, and I wasn't upset with her. We were both infuriated with him.

I asked her, "What do we do?"

She suggested that I try calling him again on his cell phone and that we set him up. We wanted to see what he had to say. I called her from my cell phone, put her on hold, and then called his phone. He picked up, and then I reconnected with her.

"Matthew, where are you?" I asked. "I've been trying to reach you."

"Oh, I was just out getting a bite to eat."

I said, "Well, I really miss you. I just wanted to catch up and talk. Are you by yourself?"

He said, "Of course, I'm by myself!" He continued playfully, "Who else would I be with?"

I responded, "Oh, I just wanted to make sure. I know you told me in Spain that you really loved me, and you wanted to have children, and to me, that meant someday you might want to get married. Are you sure that's still what you want? And I'm the one for you?"

"Of course you are," he said. "Why are you acting this way?"

"Because I am here too," said Stephannie.

There was a long pause on the phone line, finally Matthew yelled, "I can't believe you two set me up!"

"Set you up?" I responded. "What about leading both of us on?"

He hung up the phone on us. I called the hotel back, and Stephannie and I chatted. We were mortified and enraged. As we were talking, I could hear Matthew come into their hotel room. Stephannie set down the phone, but she didn't hang it up all the way. I could hear them talking.

Matthew said, "Stephannie, how could you set me up like that!"

"How dare you put this on me!" Stephannie yelled. "You have a girlfriend that you were in Spain with, talking about having children with and living with her while she goes to school! I would say that is serious, Matthew!"

"All that was before I saw you this time. I realize now how I feel about you."

Stephannie asked, "And just how do you feel?"

"Well, earlier, you mentioned you wanted to get married, so you still want to?"

Stephannie said, "I don't know, Matthew. I'm not sure I can really trust you anymore. I need to think about it."

After a pause, I heard Matthew slam the door of the hotel room.

I was numb. What just happened? I couldn't believe my ears. *Was everything he said in Spain untrue? How could I be so blind?* I cried myself to sleep that night, knowing I was going to have to face him the next day at work. *What would I say to him?*

I had to put on my professional face the next day and be a happy medical assistant. I didn't say more than necessary to Matthew other than what the patient needed. I was saving it all for the end of the day.

The last patient of the day was a friend of his. I was in the exam room next to them, cleaning it, and I could overhear them talking. His friend was talking about me to Matthew.

He said, "Oh, she's nothing but a bitch. Just let her go. She can't mean that much to you."

Matthew responded, "But I really do like her."

His slimy friend continued by reminding him about all the women he could have, "You have so many after you!"

Matthew kept defending me, which made me feel a little better. It was all I could do to stop myself from walking into that room and slapping the patient. He finally left the room. It was time for Matthew and me to talk.

I decided I was not going to be second in anyone's life. It was either going to be Stephannie or me. I told Matthew, "Take the weekend to think about this and let me know."

He said, "I don't have to think about it. I want you. I don't know what I was thinking. I was living in the past with her. I want a future with you!"

I said, "Okay, if you really mean it, then call her right now. Put her on speaker so I can hear, and tell her it is over."

He pulled out his cell phone and dialed her phone number. "Hello?" she said.

"Hi, Stephannie, it is Matthew. I am so sorry I put you through so much last night. I have decided to move on and be with Addy. I am so sorry I misled you."

There was silence at the end of the phone line.

She finally said, "You better be sure because I don't give second chances."

Matthew said, "Yes, I am sure."

He hung up the phone. There was a stillness in the room. We both sat there in silence for what seemed to me an eternity. I didn't even want to hug him or thank him. I had a horrible feeling in my stomach. He finally did hug me, but I really didn't hug him back. I told him I had to get some sleep since I hadn't slept all night.

"Matthew, it will take me some time to get over this."

I went home that night and prayed to God that I was doing the right thing in letting this man back into my life. My heart told me one thing, but my gut was twisted in knots.

Eventually, we got past this, and I started trusting him again. But it took a long time. Matthew was really good at turning on the charm and reeling me back in quickly. I did love him, so naturally, I forgave him.

The day had finally come for me to move to our apartment. We packed up my car, and I said goodbye to my family and my sweet daughter, Nicole. My plan was to come home each weekend to visit her.

Matthew and I moved into our apartment that weekend, and I started at Duke the following Monday.

2000–2002

Twenty-Four Months at Duke

The train ride was great. It took me forty-five minutes to get to campus. Matthew would drop me off before he went to work with Dr. Ellis and then pick me up after work.

Duke's schedule was intense. On the first day of orientation, they told us to look around at the other forty-nine people in the room.

"This is your family now," they told us. "Say goodbye to your real family. Tell them you will see them in twenty-four months. You all need each other, or you will never make it through this program. We encourage you to find classmates of a different discipline and form study groups. Some of you will fail. Some of you will feel like you are failing. Some of you will get divorced, and some of you may even experience a death in your family, but you will make it through this only if you put your heart and soul into it."

Wow, that was a lot to take in.

Every day we sat in lecture after lecture all day long. There were so many notes. I would record them all and then go home and type them out, organizing them onto note cards and highlighting their most important parts. I'd stay up until 2:00 a.m. eating peperoncini and Cheez-Its just to try and stay awake. Every Monday we had an exam. This was just the first quarter.

Matthew was supposed to oversee cooking. I soon learned the only thing he knew how to cook was steak. As he put it, "But I'm really good at it!" Because of this, I had a lot of Top Ramen and take-out food.

The money was not coming in as Matthew had promised. He said his ventures were coming along but not as fast as he thought they would. "They will soon!" he would say.

I continued to take funds out of my 401(k) to pay my tuition and our rent. I also wanted Nicole to have something in case of an emergency. I got an offer in the mail for a $25,000 credit card, so I decided to activate it. Matthew saw the card on the counter and asked about it. After I told him its purpose, he mentioned it would be nice if he had something like that too.

"I am a little short on cash, and it would be nice to have something in case of an emergency."

I said, "Okay, but only for that!" He agreed.

Duke continued to be taxing, and the next quarter we went to our preceptor sites for three weeks. This is where PA students would shadow patients after a few weeks. By the fourth week, we returned to campus and had an exam every Monday. I could still remember that nauseous feeling every week. It's still there when I drove by the campus years later. I had no idea how difficult this would be, and neither did my classmates, but we helped one another. Matthew continued to help me and answered all my questions at night when I was studying.

I visited Nicole on the weekends, but even then, I had to study. She was in her senior year of high school and was often out and about with her friends most days. This helped for sure. Prom was coming up, and she was busy planning for the event. They were very excited and wanted to rent a bus to take them to and from the event.

"Mom, this could actually make us money!" she bargained. "We are going to charge more than the bus cost and put the money we make in the bank account for our class reunions!"

She and Tina had it all planned out. I thought it was a brilliant idea. Not only was it cheap, but it was also safe—just in case any of them were drinking alcohol. This way, none of them would be driving.

Nicole said, "There is just one favor I need. Can we please put the deposit on your credit card? We will pay you back once we collect the money!"

Nicole was always very responsible with money, so I agreed.

Matthew and I went back to our apartment that Sunday night because I had class Monday morning and another one of those dreadful exams. I did pretty well, but luckily, I typically always did well on those. That night I took the train home as usual. When I got to the station, Matthew wasn't there to pick me up. I tried calling his cell phone, but it went to voice mail. I waited for fifteen minutes and tried again, but still no answer. So I started walking. I was carrying my backpack with all my heavy books. Being it was 2000, before electronic books and the rise of laptops, everything was paper based, and medical books were huge! It took me forty-five minutes to walk home from the train station that evening. Just as I walked through the door, the phone rang. I threw my backpack on the floor to quickly answered. It was Nicole on the other end, and she was hysterical.

"Mom, your credit card was declined, and now we can't get the bus!"

I said, "That's impossible. I have $25,000 credit on that card. Let me call the bank and find out what is going on."

I got on the line with a bank representative who informed me that Matthew Alden had gone into the bank that day and withdrawn $25,000 as a cash advance on the card. My heart sank to the bottom of my stomach. *Where was he? Who was he with? Did he take my money and leave me?* I tried calling his cell again, and still, it went straight to voice mail.

In the meantime, I had to help Nicole. I felt horrible that all her plans for prom would be ruined because I trusted Matthew. I called my mom and told her my credit card was missing, and I had reported it stolen. There was no way I could tell her the truth. She would be so angry with Matthew. I asked if she could give Nicole her credit card, and she agreed.

My stomach was once again in knots. I couldn't eat. I couldn't focus on my studies. *Where was he?* All those emotions with

Stephannie came flooding back. Finally, he came home around nine thirty that evening. I was livid.

"Where have you been?" I yelled.

"I was busy after work with my business venture. Time got away from me."

"You didn't have the decency to even call me and tell me? I had to walk home from the train station by myself! And to make matters worse, Nicole tried to use the charge card for her bus for prom, and it was declined because you went into the bank today and withdrew $25,000 on it!" I was screaming by this point. The veins on my neck were about to burst. "What did you do with the money, Matthew? I want it back! Every bit of it!" I was running toward him by now. "I told you it was only for an emergency! What was the emergency?"

He lifted his hands and seemingly braced himself against my wrath. "I used it for my business venture, the prototypes one I told you about. I promise you it will pay off."

I tried to calm myself down. Catching my breath for a moment, I asked him, "Who is this that you are helping, and why?"

He then proceeded to tell me about a famous guy who was well accomplished in building new medical prototypes in the medical industry. "I am helping him get restarted. His name is Dr. Rob Williamson. He is well-known for making these prototypes. I was meeting with him to get things going. I gave him that money to get the ball rolling." He tried to explain the science of these prototypes, but it was way over my head. I had no idea what he was talking about or what they did! For all I knew, maybe he made the whole thing up.

I tried to reason with him. "Matthew, that still doesn't sit well with me. That was for emergencies, and this was not an emergency! That money was mine, not yours." I got close to him, lowering my voice and gritting my teeth. "You are going to pay every penny of that back to me!"

He responded, "Oh, I will, and even more! You will see, Addy."

I went to bed that night with my back turned away from Matthew, and my stomach once again twisted in knots. I quietly prayed to God. It was the same prayer as just a while ago with Stephannie. *Am I doing the right thing, God? Please give me a sign.*

The next day, I had to put aside the previous day's dramatic events and focus on my studies. It was then that the program announced we would have our first practicum at the end of the month. A practicum happened every quarter where a student went into a room with an actor who pretended to be a patient. The session was recorded, and a professor sat in the corner, taking notes through-out, marking down your scores as the exam was in progress. As the "PA," you were expected to come into the room and act just as you would if it were a real patient. There's no preparation or prewarning. The patient/actor's "chief complaint" could be anything. To add even more pressure, you were being timed throughout the whole event. Once you finished with the questioning and examining, you then left to go into another room where you had fifteen minutes to write up your assessment and plan.

Duke was very strict in the first quarter of school. You weren't allowed to use abbreviations for anything. For example, if I were to listen to someone's heart, I could not put *RRR*, which in medicine was a common abbreviation for "regular, rate, and rhythm." You had to write out the words *regular, rate, and rhythm.* For the lungs, the abbreviated *CTA* would have to be fully written as *clear to ausculta-tion.* This was the same for every body part you examined on that patient. It was probably the most stressful time for all of us as students. I could remember there being a long line outside the restroom as we each awaited our turn to be called into the pseudoexam room to complete our practicum. You either had diarrhea or you were vomiting. *And believe me, that wasn't abbreviated either.*

My apartment was the headquarters for rehearsing practicums. All my study partners would come to my house and practice for hours. I had the best and most unique group of study partners. It consisted of an ER nurse, a paramedic, a respiratory therapist, another medical assistant like me, a physical therapist, an exercise physiologist, and a physician from Russia. Matthew did come in handy for this part as well. He loved to teach, and he was really good at it. He had a talent for explaining things in a way you could understand them easily. It was just like his chemistry lessons with Nicole. When any of us had questions, he was more than willing to help.

Dr. Ellis was supposed to be my preceptor, but a lot of times, he was too busy to help me. That's when he would ask Matthew to take over.

No one in the office knew we were dating or even living together at this point. It was an uncomfortable situation. Matthew didn't seem to mind it, and he was a wonderful teacher, but I was afraid that if anyone at Duke found out, I might get in trouble. *How could this not be considered a conflict of interest?*

My study partners knew he was sometimes helping as a preceptor. Somehow one of the other students in my class found out and reported it to the dean for a conflict of interest. My heart sank when I was called to the dean. *Who would report me, and why?* I was confronted by the dean and asked if Dr. Alden was my preceptor.

I carefully responded, "No. Dr. Ellis is my preceptor. Sometimes he is too busy, and he asks Dr. Alden to fill in for him."

She then asked, "Is it true he is your boyfriend and you two are living together?"

I blushed and responded with a quiet, "Yes."

She sighed and continued, "Well, Addy, you know this is against our regulations. This will have to be brought up with the board, and we will decide what type of discipline will be taken against you. It may take a couple of weeks before we get back to you."

"I understand," I replied. I followed it up with a sincere apology and went on to say, "My actions were not intentional. It was just the circumstances of my original preceptor not following through with his obligations."

I left her office with that same twisted feeling in the pit of my stomach. This was becoming an all too familiar sensation. *Okay, God. Here we go again. What secretive, mysterious lesson are You trying to teach me now?*

I sat down on the bench outside the dean's office and sobbed. I had worked so hard to get here. Could everything be over just like that? After a minute, I gave my best effort to regain composure and put myself back together. I had to get back to class.

I slipped back into my seat next to my closest friend, Charlene. She whispered in my ear, "Is everything okay? You look like you have been crying."

I said, "I'll tell you during the break."

"Okay," she responded.

When I finally told her what had happened, she was livid.

"Why would anyone do this to you? You know what! Someone that is very jealous of you, that's who!"

I didn't have an answer. I was just broken.

She continued, "Do you remember when the class was deciding about who should be class president and everyone wanted you to do it? Roberta wanted so badly to be it. Remember that?"

"Yes," I responded. "But I told everyone I didn't want it."

Charlene said, "I know, but she never liked the idea that everyone wanted you and not her."

I thought hard about what she was saying. Something didn't add up.

"How would she have found out about Matthew and me?"

Charlene said, "Well, she and Liz are roommates, and Liz is in our practicum study group. Maybe she mentioned something to Roberta, not really knowing this would happen." Charlene leaned forward and grabbed my hand, "I think we should ask her."

I let out a frustrated sigh. "Man! I thought high school was over!"

We found Liz studying on a bench outside and approached her. I softly called out to her, "Hi, Liz. Sorry to bother you. I just have a quick question. Did you happen to mention anything about Matthew helping me out as a preceptor to anybody? Don't worry. I wouldn't be mad at you if you did."

Liz responded, "I might have. Why?"

I told her what had happened with the dean. She was furious.

"That sounds like something Roberta would do! She mentioned that she didn't think it was right that you had a doctor for a boyfriend, and he could help you. She said it wasn't fair to everyone else." She looked up at me, frowning. "I am so sorry, Addy."

"It's okay, Liz. I know you didn't do it on purpose. Thank you for telling me."

When Matthew picked me up at the train station that night, I told him what had happened. He couldn't believe how petty Roberta had been and that Duke would dismiss me for something like this.

"We'll hire an attorney and fight it if they do," he said.

"Right," I retorted. "And with what money?"

The only thing I could do was pray at this point. Like so many things so far in my life, I simply had to leave it in God's hands.

I finished that hellish week at Duke and was looking forward to my next three weeks of rotation at the free clinic. I volunteered there for several years before I was accepted into PA school. It was a familiar place with familiar faces.

When I arrived on my first day, it was like a homecoming. Everyone was so pleasant there. Because I had worked there for so long, everyone knew me. For this go-around, Dr. Drake was my new preceptor. He was an amazing teacher. He was hard on me at times, but I learned so much from him. As a student, you would go see the patient, then come into the doctor's lounge and tell your preceptor all about your patient. It is called presenting your patient. You would tell your preceptor what the patient told you, what they were complaining about, and what you found on the exam if you had an idea of their problem or diagnosis. You also had to list differentials and what else you thought might be the problem or diagnosis. If I ever mixed up my presentation with him, he would make me start all over again and only give me thirty seconds to finish it. The first week I would only see a handful of patients, but as the weeks progressed, you were expected to see more.

I continued my rotations with Dr. Ellis and Matthew. They were both excellent preceptors. Matthew was very patient with me and was never demeaning. He would say things like, "That's a good thought, Adeline, but instead, what about..." I was completely wrong at times, but he would never make me feel inadequate or that I had no idea what I was talking about. Instead, he had a gentle way of making you feel good about yourself despite your mistakes.

One afternoon he thought he was doing me a favor by giving me a seventeen-year-old for a physical exam.

"This will be easy," he told me.

Apparently, seventeen-year-olds didn't have much going on, so it was a slam dunk. The boy came in complaining about a sore throat as well as wanting a complete physical. I went through my typical questions at the beginning. Once I got to the sexual exam, I asked if he was sexually active.

With a quick response, he answered, "Yes."

I continued with my required follow-up, "With men, women, or both?" I always said this in one sentence and fast so I didn't embarrass the patient.

Again, quickly, he answered, "Yes."

Definitely not what I was expecting. Okay, next question.

"How many partners have you had?"

Here he finally took a moment before answering. After a brief pause, he said, "I think about twenty or so."

It was all I could do to contain myself. "Um, did you use protection?" I asked.

"No," he said.

As the story went on, I learned more about this teenager than I had ever wanted. He and his brother had been in France, where they rented an RV. Throughout their stay, they hosted rave parties, having the time of their lives all summer long. I had to ask the typical questions about what type of sex he had had. It was everything. He answered yes to penetrative, oral, and anal. All I could think of was, *Dear God, I hope my daughter knows more than this seventeen-year-old.* I also couldn't stop thinking to myself that Matthew had just given me a very difficult patient! The moral of the story here, nothing was a slam dunk but a slam dunk!

The patient ended up having chlamydia of the throat and gonorrhea of the anus and tested positive for HIV. It was one of the most difficult phone calls I had ever made to a patient. Later, I didn't share the name of the patient with my daughter out of confidentiality, but I did tell her the story. I'd never forget the look on her face.

With an awe-like expression, she asked, "Why didn't they tell us in sex ed that you could get things like that from oral sex!" Oops…

Most nights were spent studying, and when possible, my weekends were devoted to Nicole. By the end of Sunday, I was back cramming for another round of tests that took place on the first Monday of every month. Again with the Mondays! It felt like Groundhog Day.

When I returned to campus that next week, I was called back to the dean's office. Buried in my work, I had forgotten about the issue until that very moment. My palms were sweating, and my head was spinning as I walked slowly to the office. Would they really disenroll me? Could I fight this? Could Dr. Ellis explain why he asked Matthew to fill in for him? All these thoughts were racing through my head. Maybe if I cried profusely and told them how hard I worked to get into the program, they would show me mercy.

I was told to wait in the waiting area, and the dean would be with me shortly. It seemed like an eternity. It was only a few minutes.

"Adeline, please come in and have a seat." She took a deep breath and said, "Well, the board met last week, and we discussed your case. After reviewing your file and grades at length, we have reached a conclusion. Addy, it was unanimous…" She paused, and I felt the air get sucked out of the room. Then she cracked a small grin and continued, "You are one of our best students. So whatever you are doing, keep doing it!" But tell Dr. Ellis to step up to the plate.

I immediately started crying. It wasn't the painful tears I had prepared in the waiting room, though. No, these were tears of joy!

I blurted out as I reached for her hand, "Oh, Dean Phillips! Thank you so much."

I left her office and immediately called Matthew to tell him the good news.

He said, "I told you this would work out! But if it didn't, I would have hired the best lawyer for you."

I hung up the phone and thought, *Sure. With what money, Matthew? Mine?* Even though the news had me elated, I still couldn't resist the urge to throw shade at him about my financial situation. Matthew still had not been helping. He did give me a couple hundred dollars from his paycheck every few weeks, but it was nothing like he had promised me from the beginning. Regardless, he continued with his business meetings at night and was always on the phone.

I went back to class and told Charlene and Liz the good news from the dean. They were so relieved and happy for me. I had no doubt that when Liz told Roberta, she was disappointed in the outcome. But I really didn't care.

Eight hours of lectures five days a week was grueling. I was still recording all the lectures while also taking written notes. I felt like a total nerd. But this was what helped me get through college, and I was certain it would help me at Duke too. It was so much information to process.

I remembered Matthew saying at the beginning of my program, "You are learning in twenty-four months what I learned in four years."

When the rest of the class found out I was typing out the class notes, they began to ask me for copies. I was happy to share. I carried those note cards everywhere I went. Anytime I had a spare moment, I pulled them out and studied. I studied on the train, on my lunch, and yes, even in the bathroom! Most of my classmates did too, especially for the practicums.

For those twenty-four months, my life was consumed by Duke, my classmates, study sessions, tape recorders, note cards, peperoncini, Cheez-Its, and a seemingly endless supply of Top Ramen soup for lunch every day. I lived on three to four hours of sleep every night, rode the train back and forth every day, and all the while still wondered if Matthew would be there to pick me up at night. It wasn't long before I started dipping into my savings for school tuition and rent for both my places. It had taken me so long to get here. I finally saw the light at the end of the tunnel. I knew it would all be worth it. I couldn't wait to practice medicine. I often reflected on those days at Pashupatinath. I was still so thankful to the Missionaries of Charity and the gift they gave to me. Who would have thought now, nearly twelve years later, it was all coming true? I'd fought, scratched, clawed, and wrestled my way through it to the end. And now I was about to emerge victorious. And bigger—I gained twenty-three pounds in those twenty-four months!

2002

Conquering the Beast, aka Graduation

January 18, 2002, I finally completed my program at Duke and prepared to walk across the aisle. Completely immersed in my studies and routine, I didn't find until right before commencement that I would graduate with honors. I had been so focused and determined that it took a classmate informing me in passing that I was at the top of the class. This was huge to me. After the many battles I fought to reach this point, it was an even greater win to know I'd wear the bright-yellow satin sash over my gown signifying I graduated with honors.

The commencement day arrived, and I stood with the few graduates who had also received honors in our class. My head was high, and my shoulders seemed to sit back more than normal. I was so proud of what I had done. After graduation was over, Matthew and I wanted to put a small celebration together. Money was incredibly tight, and there simply wasn't enough to do anything large. Instead, we hosted an intimate reception with a few friends and my family to attend.

The event was embarrassing. Virtually all my savings had been spent on my education and the rent payment for our apartment. The event's budget was basically nothing. Matthew had yet to pay me back for the money he spent on his venture, and we barely had enough to put some food on the table for our guests. About twenty minutes into the reception, we ran out of food. Most of my guests either ate very little or did not at all. I was a PA student, freshly graduated with honors from Duke, and I couldn't even afford to feed my family.

But we celebrated. I had done it. Before the night ended, Matthew revealed his gift to me. It was a beautiful glass plaque that showed my name, an indication that I was on the dean's List, and a lovely quote from a famous doctor of old.

It was thoughtful and precious to me. An embodiment of the struggles I faced, obstacles I overcame, and the new future I was able to uncover. My dreams of being a physician assistant had been realized, and I now had the chance to steer my life in a better direction.

2002—expensive nuptials and costly consequences

Shortly after I graduated, Matthew surprised me with a marriage proposal. It was a perfect cap to an already perfect year. By this time, Nicole was in college, so we scheduled our wedding for later in the year when she was home. Having been married once before, I wasn't looking for a large, outlandish ceremony with all the thrills and frills. A more intimate setting with our closest friends and family was all I needed, not to mention that it was cheaper. Freshly graduated, I hadn't recouped the money I'd spent on college quite, and Matthew had yet to pay his debt to me back. Still, the bills, rent, and charges never stopped. It would take a while before I saw the financial gain of my hard work.

But Matthew demanded the big wedding. Up to this point, he wasn't even sure he would ever get married. But now he was, and he wanted everything just perfect. The ceremony was to be held at a large, beautiful church in New York City. The decorations were top-notch, and the wedding party was to be clad in full tuxes and beautiful dresses.

Matthew insisted on glamour and more intimate details as well. For my wedding dress, he specifically requested I buy one with a very long train and thick veil that covered my face. As a romantic by nature, he had envisioned the long train reaching down the church aisle and him slowly lifting the veil to reveal my face for our first kiss. Romantic indeed, but like most beautiful things, it was very pricey. The demands for elegance didn't stop there. Before we knew it, we had a pipe organ, a singer, and several violin players all playing together (basically a small orchestra)—and priced separately—as I made my grand entrance. It was beautiful. The same musicians played as we exited the cathedral as husband and wife. People remarked we looked like Brad Pitt and Jennifer Anniston coming down the aisle! What a nice compliment.

Despite the cost, the wedding had wonderful, memory-making moments. Lifelong friends of mine were able to participate. My close friend, Deirdre, had offered to do my hair and makeup along with all my bridesmaids. She had always been thoughtful and generous in the thirty-plus years I had known her. She made me feel extra special for the day.

We filled the stage with nine groomsmen and nine bridesmaids, all dressed the same in a beautifully coordinated event. The reception afterward was just as nice, and our many guests all remarked on the grandeur of it all.

The only catch was we had no money for any of it. Instead, we borrowed money to put on the wedding. This became a common theme where Matthew was concerned. His dreams were often larger than his pocketbook, but still, he made it work.

Matthew's family wasn't keen on the idea of him getting married, and frankly, neither were some of mine. Having lived his life as a proud bachelor with no strings attached, many on his side of the aisle weren't convinced of this show of commitment. This became clear to me when some of his friends decided to show up. Through their discussions with our guests, it was confirmed that the only reason they had attended was to see if it would actually occur. At this time, I was too mesmerized by it all to truly listen to this message. To me, it was less of a warning and more of a friendly jab at a longtime friend.

But he did it. We said "I do" and vowed to live a life full of loyalty, commitment, and fidelity together "until death does us part."

Shortly after the wedding bells stopped ringing, Matthew revealed in the privacy of our new marriage that he owed a lot of people money. Obviously, this was a shock. He reluctantly informed me that he hadn't kept up his student loan repayment from medical school, owed quite a bit in back taxes, and had maxed out five credit cards. With more than $250,000 in looming debt, I panicked. But after shaking off the initial shock of it all, I researched and found that there were ways to negotiate smaller payoffs for credit companies. After calling the card companies, I was able to reduce the total amount to $25,000 and pay off the cards. We did this with the help of my mother. Thankfully, she had excellent credit and was always offered opportunities to transfer balances on her credit cards for reduced rates. I promised her we would pay her back every dime and take over the monthly payment to the credit card company.

For the student loans, there was no negotiation. We reached out to Matthew's father and asked if he would give us a loan. With us barely making ends meet, I worked with him to set up a payment arrangement, promising that we would pay it in full once we started making money in our practice. Years later, when we were far more financially stable, I paid every cent to him, staying true to my word.

Then there were the back taxes. Where credit negotiations and well-off in-laws were one thing, the IRS was an entirely separate issue. Matthew and I searched high and low for a company that would assist us in managing the back payments. Thankfully we found one that worked with the IRS and allowed us to make reasonable payments.

We managed to climb out of the chasm that Matthew had brought with him, but the pain of knowing how much was hidden, only to later be revealed after it was too late, hung around like a stench that wouldn't go away. Over time, it dulled, but I couldn't seem to shake what had happened. All I could do was simply store it away and try and distract myself from the better part of life. But the next months would mean struggle and grind with a glimmer of light at the far end.

2003

Careers and Curveballs

When the wedding was over, Matthew and I were officially married and turned our sights on standing up our careers.

Postgraduation, I managed to work three separate jobs in order to make ends meet and begin my career in medicine. The free clinic where I did my PA rotation asked to hire me. My hire at the clinic was a first for them. Never before, and never since, had they hired a PA to provide medical service for their patients. To this day, I was the only one. I also continued to support Matthew in his practice as his office patient list continued to grow. The other job was a short stint at Planned Parenthood, where I provided medical services for their local office as well as working with their offshoot program SAGE— Standing Against Global Exploitation.

This became a truly remarkable experience for me and an eye-opening introduction to medicine and patient care. SAGE was primarily housed downtown in the local mission, where former prostitutes sought medical assistance related to their many health issues. Most of the women were addicted to heroin after being exposed to it by their johns.

The strict Catholic schoolgirl in me was absolutely shocked by what I witnessed. These poor women were ailing and often reeling from some of the worst bodily responses you'd imagine that could come from this lifestyle, particularly in the early 2000s when there was little to no assistance for them. Often, I'd need to draw blood from my patients only to find out that their veins had shriveled to unrecognizable levels due to the constant abuse they received from needle jabs. Often, I'd rely on them to show me where the best vein was for injection. If the arms or hands weren't available, sometimes I could be found drawing blood from between their toes.

The mission was in the heart of North Carolina, Wadesboro. Since it catered to women, no men were allowed in the facility. Matthew would attempt to bring me lunch at times, meeting me in the alleyway next to the entrance. I'd never forget witnessing this tall beast of a man cower in the corner as he scanned his surroundings, fearing for his safety.

"I can't believe you work here, Addy!" he'd whisper as I grabbed my lunch from him.

"Matthew, this is where these ladies live."

After I'd take the lunch, he'd scurry away back to his car and leave before having to face the throes of mankind.

I originally started at another location, an area known for its prostitution. I couldn't imagine a more interesting and, at times, alarming way to practice medicine. So often I'd be faced with questions that I would have never thought a woman needed to ask. There were moments when these women, who had devoted, whether willingly or not, their entire bodies to their job, were clueless about their safety and hygiene. One woman even asked me which "hole" the john needed to enter first! I was both appalled and heartbroken for these ladies, and the more I worked with them, the more my compassion for others was rekindled as before.

My stay at Planned Parenthood began to dwindle as the local free clinic requested that I work more hours for them. Matthew's practice also began to take off around this time, and I was needed there more to assist with the new patients. It came to a point quickly that I could only spare approximately three half days with the clinic to allow more time to devote to Matthew's practice.

Matthew practice was growing with new patients, but he still needed more work. He applied for a job serving as an instructor at the local collage. Matthew, being an outstanding doctor and teacher, would be perfect for the role. He easily got the job. Between the two jobs, it helped supplement our income.

Before long, Matthew and I began to see that our finances had shifted in the right direction. Between Matthew's two jobs and my three, suddenly we had money in the bank to pay our bills without starving ourselves. Though we were by no means well-off, we had enough to get by, and things were looking up.

Matthew's practice was growing rapidly due to his many established relationships from his time with Dr. Ellis. This became an issue after a while. Many of those patients loved Matthew so much that they decided to leave Dr. Ellis's practice to follow him. As could be expected, Dr. Ellis was furious at Matthew. He went on a rampage, completely separating himself from Matthew and me. I was heartbroken as I couldn't understand why he was so mad at me. What had I done?

At one point, we passed each other in the hospital when I asked him candidly to answer that question. His response was curt and emotional. Essentially, he informed me that Matthew had betrayed him, but I had abandoned him. I reminded him that my goal the whole time was to pursue a medical degree.

"Yes, but then you left me, Addy!" he responded.

"I had to, Dr. Ellis! I needed to follow Matthew," I tried to explain.

His next words were chilling. Leaning in, he told me that he didn't trust Matthew and that one day I'd regret following him. Then without another word, he left me in the hallway. This conversation only confused me more. I'd regret following Matthew. But he loved Matthew! What changed?

It was clear that Dr. Ellis had seen something in Matthew I had yet to notice. Something nefarious, manipulative. I was too high on life to believe it then. How could this man, whom I had just pledged to live out my years building a life, turn out to be a monster like Dr. Ellis thought he was? It was clearly foolish.

I left that day upset at the lost relationship but excited about the budding future that Matthew and I were building. Great things were on the horizon, and I could see we were only getting started.

At the time, we were renting space in another doctor's office. Money was better, but still far too tight to open our own office. But the business was booming. Eventually, Matthew's patient list grew large, and the word was getting out about this amazing doctor whom his clients adored.

Among those enamored clients was an older couple named John and Louise Langham. After choosing to follow Matthew into his practice, they fell head over heels in love with both of us. Fully convinced that our practice would change the city, they began referring us to their wealthy friends and essentially marketing for us among the geriatric crowd. As this was Matthew's specialty, the assistance was much appreciated.

As the year progressed, I noticed a small callous-like spot on the roof of my mouth. It seemed to come out of nowhere and was no larger than the size of a dime. Uncertain as to what it was, I went to my dentist for a checkup and to ask him for his opinion. After examination, he couldn't seem to determine what it was but figured it was infection related. He placed me on antibiotics and referred me to an endodontist for a second opinion. The specialist was also confused and referred me once more to a head, nose, and throat surgeon.

When the ENT surgeon examined the spot, he, too, was stumped as to what it might be but decided it was clearly something that didn't belong. He scheduled surgery to have it removed.

During this time, I called Nicole to make her aware of my procedure. Considering that all three doctors were certain it was nothing major and Nicole was away at college, I told her not to be concerned and stay where she was. She came anyway. A few days later, the surgeon prepped me and put me under, then began removing the curious spot from the roof of my mouth. Moments later, when I came to the hospital recovery room, my surgeon met me at my bedside with a frown on his face.

"Addy, I'm sorry to tell you this, but when we began to remove the lesion, it was clear that the spot was a rare form of hard palate cancer known as polymorphous low-grade adenocarcinoma."

I was stunned. What was supposed to be a routine procedure ended up becoming a diagnosis of cancer. Of course, the surgeon had already informed Matthew and Nicole, who had been waiting in the family visiting room. Nicole was extremely upset. How could she not? No one had prepared her for this outcome. No one could have expected this to happen.

The surgeon went on to explain that the dime-sized spot was just the surface. The full area that was removed from the roof of my mouth was roughly the size of a silver dollar. He then informed me that he would send my biopsy slides off to Mt. Sinai to determine if he'd gotten clean margins, meaning all cancer had been removed. He was confident that was the case but agreed to the second opinion.

After a month of waiting with no results, I visited the surgeon again for a post-op checkup, only to ask him once more if my slides had been reviewed.

Quite passively, as if to appease me, he offered up a simple response, "Oh, they came back. You're fine. You had clean margins."

I felt instant relief. "So does this mean I don't need chemo or radiation?" I asked.

"Right, you're good. We got it all," was his final response.

Somewhat skeptical of the doctor's nonchalant answer, I still did my best to appreciate my prognosis. What could have been much worse turned out to be a small blip on my timeline, and I was free to carry on with my dreams. I rushed home that evening to let Matthew know the results. Him being in the medical field much longer than me, he was equally skeptical of the doctor's response minus the ability to move past it. He asked if I'd be willing to have a second opinion from a friend of his in oncology. I agreed only to settle his nerves and frankly because I wasn't too happy with my surgeon's handling of my situation.

Matthew connected me with Dr. Jennifer Greer, who agreed to look over my charts and offer another glimpse at my results. A few days later, I received a call from her. She was seething on the other end of the phone.

"Addy, I am so mad," she began. "I've never been more disappointed at another colleague before."

She then informed me that when she visited pathology to reassess Mt. Sinai's results of my slides, she realized that they were still sitting in the office, having never been sent in the first place.

I was confused and furious. The surgeon had insisted that he not only sent my slides to Mt. Sinai but that they had informed him my margins were clear. For a few days now, I had been convinced I was cancer-free, and now I found that no one, not even my surgeon, could be sure that's the case. Dr. Greer agreed to follow through with the slides and requested Mt. Sinai to review them quickly.

In a few short days, the results came back. Not only was cancer still there, but it also had spread to the palatine nerve, which led from the mouth to the brain. My life was in danger, and this doctor hadn't the time to care for me fully.

My case was then brought before the tumor board at the hospital to determine the best course of action. The same surgeon who so easily dismissed my case was the one who needed to now present my results. Having been caught in a clear lack of true medical attention, he chose to lie and say that though he did receive clear margins, he had had a change of heart, deciding it was best for me to have radiation—just to be safe.

The truth was much more revealing, but the reality was this: I finally could get the treatment I needed. Thus, at the start of 2004, I began my journey for three months, receiving thirty-seven total radiation treatments over the course of fifty-five days. The doctors for my care agreed that in order to reduce the chance of recurrence, they would isolate the treatment to my palate. This meant that I would need to lay still for ten to fifteen minutes at a time, my head bolted on a table and a mask over my face as the radioactive poison was administered to my mouth. It was agonizing. I felt like I was Hannibal Lecter. The mask, the straight jacket, even the horror of it all. Nicole insisted on sitting with me for one of my appointments. I have no doubt she regretted it afterward.

Naturally, the effects of the radiation were, at times, severe. In three months, I lost fifteen pounds and suffered regular bouts of fatigue and sickness. For my already thinner frame, losing any more weight was significant. The Langhams, seeing the toll my treatments were taking on Matthew and me, decided to step up and offer us to move in with them. They lived right beside the hospital and were more than willing to take me to and from my treatments. We gladly accepted the offer as I was struggling. The bouts of sickness and painful blisters inside my mouth made it impossible for me to eat. Steadily losing weight at an alarming pace, my doctors were prepared to put a feeding tube in me just to keep me nourished. My radiation oncologist finally came up with an oral painkiller concoction that could assist. The treatment was quite intensive. Essentially it was a mixture of lidocaine and cocaine, administered as a paste on a Q-tip to the blistering lesions in my mouth left behind from the radiation. If it worked, the pain would be numbed just long enough for me to down some Prosure/Ensure. The prescription was faxed to a compounding pharmacy.

Once I arrived, they informed me that my insurance plan wouldn't cover the prescription. I thought this was hilarious. The insurance company was more than willing to cover a PEG feeding tube to be surgically inserted in my stomach, but a simple numbing cream was out of the question. Thankfully, the self-pay option wasn't astronomical, and I agreed to pay out of pocket. But if it worked, I would be able to manage liquids. Once applied, the pain ceased just long enough, and thankfully I was able to wrestle down liquid protein, stopping my doctors from taking more drastic measures.

2004–2006

Main Office

Through everything, the Langhams remained angels in our lives. Having money to spend and the heart to give it away, they offered to support our practice by assisting in the purchase of our very own office space. Sitting in my cancer bed, I was told to search and find the right location and then piece together our office furniture. We were beside ourselves with gratitude.

As my body mended and our office was finished, we moved into our very own physical space in 2004. Thankfully the cancer treatments worked, and I was provided a clean bill of health. Matthew and I immediately went to work, looking for ways to grow our practice in the main office. By 2005, we began to build partnerships with other offices, and our office space required additional staff. We hired a receptionist, eventually adding more office staff to our team to assist with the influx of business. The times were good.

As geriatrics was our primary focus, we looked for unique ways to reach the elderly patients in the area. After much consideration, we had the idea to approach assisted living facilities, offering to set up temporary office space in their buildings and provide primary geriatric care to their patients.

Residents of these locations often fell into two different categories. On the one hand, you had those who remain independent enough to leave travel to their appointments and manage their care on their own. On the other hand, there were many patients who were more immobile and required prescriptions and care to be delivered to their apartments. Many of the second types of patients suffered from dementia or Alzheimer's or any other debilitating type of condition that confined them to a lockdown portion of the facility. As Matthew and I did our research, we found that these patients often did better when they weren't forced to change location or scenery, especially if they were ill.

This was where we knew we could be helpful. We spoke with the director of the facilities and offered to set up an on-site location, where we would essentially serve as the medical director of the program. Here we would provide primary and preventive care and any other nonspecialized medical attention that the immobile patients would require.

The plan worked, and we began to set up shop in nursing facilities around the area. The success was incredible. Not only were we seeing more patients, but the facilities were also bundling a medical director fee as a part of our agreement. As the success grew rapidly, Matthew and I realized the potential of what this type of program could do for the elderly public. Together, we created a program titled Keep in Place, or KIP. This was the new, patent-pending nomenclature for the placement of a doctor within assisted-living facilities in order to provide hands-on care for the elderly without requiring the patient to leave their apartment.

This became the first patent that Matthew and I produced together. To handle the demand, we increased our staff again by nearly tenfold. As the word got out, the medical community was impressed with the concept and its success. Matthew and I decided to offer medical training as a part of the program for PA students out of Duke. Obviously, I had familiarity with their curriculum and demands, so this became an obvious ad. We opened our services up for students to participate in geriatric rotations as a part of their school requirements. Being this was a tough niche to find, and the demand for geriatric care was so big, the school jumped at the opportunity.

2007

An Angel's Passing

My grandmother was quite a religious person. I still had visions of her walking to church in her little high heels every Sunday without fail. She was quite petite but always dressed to the nines for mass. It made her appear five times larger.

She had her hair done every Friday. There were some Sundays I had to work, and she would take Nicole with her to church. Nicole wasn't too keen on going to church, but she loved being with her GG, as she called her. Anytime Nicole was sick or I had to work, her GG babysat her. She did this from the time she was born until grade school. They had a very special bond. Nicole would have GG remind the family often that she was her favorite.

"Right, GG?" she'd add.

"Of course, my love," GG reassured. Every time.

The family would laugh and nod in agreement. This went on for years.

GG was your typical Italian grandmother. It seemed as if she always wanted you to eat something. This was the same with my great-grandmother, Nona. The first time I had a chance to visit her was when I was five years old. She served us homemade pasta that melted in my mouth. We even got to drink red wine that day! Albeit not too much, but even a sip was enough to feel twenty years older. I remembered her looking at my plate when she cleared the table.

In her broken English, she asked me, "Maria Adeline, what's the matter for you? You no *manja*." Then she added, "You too skinny." I never forgot this.

Years later, GG would teach me how to make that delicious, mouthwatering pasta from scratch. It involved a special, large wooden board. First, we'd place the flour in a mound on the board. We'd add the eggs and salt into the well that formed in the middle of the flour. Then we would whisk the eggs together with a fork, careful not to disturb the flour. We'd keep beating until each egg was fully mixed. Then using a fork, we would gently incorporate the flour into the egg mixture a little at a time until all the flour was added and it formed a ball.

It was an art form. If the mixture was too wet, it would stick to your fingers. GG taught me to rub my hands with flour and continue forming the dough. This was the trick, but once again, we had to be careful. Too much flour and we'd end up with a dry, useful ball. Then we'd have to add moisture.

It was a patient process requiring care and precision. I was honored.

After the perfect dough ball was crafted, it was time to knead. GG showed me that the easiest method involved pushing down and away from you with the palm of your hand. After one direction, you'd turn the dough ninety degrees, fold the dough over on itself, and push it down and away again. This continued until the dough was smooth. A labor of love that lasted between seven and ten minutes.

The dough was then cut into three equal parts. Each new section was balled up individually and then placed in a bowl under a towel and left to rest for fifteen minutes. Then after the small eternity passed, we'd thinly slice and roll it out with a rolling pin. The thin strips were cut, floured, and laid on a bed to dry.

The whole process took hours. When I fully inherited the recipe and was left to continue it, I purchased a pasta machine and cut the process by a few steps. But I continued to cherish the time and devotion that went into the dish. It was a steady reminder of GG. An homage to the woman who meant so much to my family.

Watching Nicole be loved by my grandmother was a beautiful testament to the many years I spent with her. The church she attended was the same one we grew up in. She loved that church. I was privileged to raise Nicole in its services. It was there she made her first holy communion and confirmation and even had her second marriage ceremony to Robert. The church didn't recognize her outdoor wedding in Italy as a blessed wedding, so Nicole agreed to host the second ceremony for GG.

This was par for the course in our home. The church was centric, important. In fact, one of the main aggressors that led to my divorcing Nicole's father was our argument over having her baptized in the Catholic church. He was against it, and I, of course, was for it. I couldn't understand why he didn't want it. We were married in the church and took our vows to raise our family in the church, but when it came time to do so, he wasn't willing. I never wanted to force religion on my child, but it was important to show her a path. This was far from the only reason we divorced, but it helped. We parted ways, and I was able to baptize Nicole at the age of five.

GG became very ill when she was in her nineties. She suffered from horrible abdominal bloating and back pain. My mom and I took her to the hospital when it became unbearable. Her doctors decided to keep her overnight for observation and to run tests the next morning to try and find the cause. There wasn't anything we could do that evening, so they told us to go home, get some rest, and come back in the morning. Reluctantly, we obliged.

The next morning, we returned to the hospital and awaited the doctors to do their rounds in her room. She was comfortable when we arrived. It was clear they had given her something for her pain. When the doctor came in, he asked who the next of kin was, and my mother spoke up. He looked at me, and I told him I was her granddaughter.

With a quick pause, he asked my mother if it was okay to speak openly about what they found. I was no amateur in medicine by now; I could tell what was happening. My heart sank as I braced for what he was going to tell us.

"Ms. Luciano, I am sorry to say this, but you have pancreatic cancer," he said quietly.

GG couldn't make sense of it at first. Like a panicked, knee-jerk reaction, I kicked into medical mode.

"Doctor, what part of the pancreas?" I asked.

"I'm sorry. Unfortunately, it is not the part we can do surgery on," he answered. "From what we can see on the scan, she is stage four."

GG really didn't understand this part.

I continued, "What can we do?"

"It's just palliation at this point," he responded. "Make her comfortable."

The air was sucked out of the room by this point. The walls were caving in, and it felt as if the curtains had grown smaller. I started feeling faint.

The doctor respectfully continued, "She has six weeks or less to live."

"No, not our GG," was all I could say. I thought she would live forever.

My mom was silent in her chair. Was she hearing this? She appeared in shock. Thoughts and emotions were swirling in my head as I tried to find a steady spot in the room. How would I tell Nicole?

The days that followed were both prescriptive and devastating.

Day 1, we arranged for her to move into a skilled nursing facility the following day, where she would have twenty-four-hour care. Hospice was brought on board. I committed to being there when we met her two hospice nurses. All GG requested was her rosary beads and her prayer book. She had been saying the rosary and her prayers daily her whole life. There was a hair salon at the skilled nursing facility. I asked if she wanted me to arrange an appointment for her, but she said no. I knew then she wasn't herself.

This woman never turned down a hair appointment. So I did her hair as best I could and put a little makeup on her.

Day 2, I met her hospice nurses. God showed His mystery again when I learned their names: Hope and Mercy. My grandmother loved it. It was a gift of comfort and familiarity. I arranged for the priest to come by and give her last rights sometime during the week.

Then it was time for the most difficult phone call of my life, Nicole. I tied to sound upbeat and encouraging, but it was difficult. She broke down immediately and started sobbing hysterically on the other end. I wanted to reach through the phone and hug her so badly. I assured her we had time and told her she needed to find a way to fly out on the weekend.

Day 3, I took every day off work going forward. I was going to be at my grandmother's bedside until the end. Her health was rapidly declining. She slept most of the time. Maybe it was the morphine? She wasn't eating much at all. Periodically, she'd wake up long enough for us to talk, or she would simply look over at me and smile. It was enough not to break down every time.

Day 4, Her abdomen was swelling larger, and she slept more than staying awake. I didn't understand how she was supposed to make it six weeks. She looked so weak. I was thankful Nicole was coming that weekend. Matthew would come to visit at night when able and bring me dinner. My mom was working and unable to take off like me, but she stopped by as much as possible.

Day 5, GG complained that her body felt like it was on fire. I started putting cold washcloths from the sink all over her frail frame. It felt like hours before the cool water finally gave her some relief. The nurses would come in and out, remarking about how wonderful of a granddaughter I was.

"Well, she would do the same for me," was my only response.

I had no clue what was going on inside her poor little body. They didn't teach me this in medical school.

Day 6, I called my brother and sister-in-law and told them they should come after work. She didn't look good. I could sense the end was coming closer. Thank goodness Nicole was coming that night. Matthew was on his way to pick her up at the airport.

That afternoon, I was working on my computer when GG sat straight up in her bed.

With a bizarre look on her face, she said, "Addy, look! In the corner!" She pointed her finger up toward the corner of the ceiling and continued, "Do you see that?"

"See what, GG?" I asked.

"The bright light!" she responded, still pointing.

"No, I don't," I answered.

She then put both her arms up toward the bright light and cried out, "Mama! Mama!" Then without another word, she lay back down and closed her eyes once again.

I was in shock. Tears began to roll down my face. Just then, my brother and sister-in-law walked into the room. I explained what had happened. They looked at me like I was delirious.

"Addy, when was the last time you ate?" my brother asked. I couldn't remember. "Please go get something to eat at the cafeteria," he continued. "We will stay with her."

Begrudgingly, I pulled myself from my chair and walked slowly to the dining hall. Not ten minutes after I found a table, my sister-in-law came to my side and sat beside me.

"Addy, I'm so sorry," she offered. "She is gone now."

"What?" I cried. "I knew it! I knew I shouldn't have left! I should have been there for her!"

Wildly, I ran down the hall and back to the room where my grandmother lay peacefully. I threw myself over her frail body and began to sob, "No, GG! Why did you go without me here?" I was in shambles. "I'm so sorry I left you!"

Just then, Nicole and Matthew walked into the room. She immediately saw me lying across GG and realized what had happened. She broke down and began to cry when she understood she wouldn't be able to say goodbye. I felt like my heart was going to explode for both of us. I told my brother to call Mom and bring as many rosaries as she had with her. She needed to call the rest of the family. Matthew called hospice and told them that she had passed, asking for them to give the family time.

My mom, her boyfriend, and my two nieces arrived with rosaries for everyone. We dimmed the lights in her room and made a circle around her bed. The whole family recited the rosary together. It was a beautiful moment, one I knew she would have loved.

At that moment, I wasn't able to think clearly about the events that occurred, but now, looking back, I knew what happened in that hospital room before GG passed. The spiritual leader Betty Bethards had once explained that when she was on the operating table, she witnessed a light calling her and her body being lifted heavenward.

She told God, "Oh no! It's not my time! Please, I have three children I still need to raise! Please put me back." The next thing she remembered was waking up in a recovery room.

I had since read of others being called by the light and by loved ones as they passed. I knew, without a shadow of a doubt, that GG was being called by my great-grandmother, Nona, her mother. I knew that in that very moment, I witnessed her spirit leave her body. I didn't miss her death. I actually witnessed it.

I thanked God every day for giving me this wonderful gift.

2007

Nicole's Journey Begins

Nicole was finishing her senior year in college, pursuing a bachelor's in broadcast journalism. By the time she graduated, our *KIP* program was expanding, and the need for more assistance was ever present. While she awaited her opportunities postgraduation, Matthew and I hired her for medical assistance in our practice. She stayed close to us, observing and taking vitals, offering support with the office, and essentially fitting in wherever we needed her. As always, she did a wonderful job.

At one point, Nicole approached Matthew and me in the office and asked if we were ready for her to present.

"What do you mean present?" I asked.

"Present! As in present my patient to you," she responded.

She then proceeded to walk through the typical medical presentation that seasoned medical students and physicians did in order for doctors to determine care for a patient. Not only did she deliver it perfectly, but it was also as if she had been doing it for years.

"Where on earth did you learn how to do that, Nicole?" I asked, surprised.

"Well, Mom, I listened."

She went on to explain that as a journalism major, one of the primary skills she obtained was the ability to observe, listen, and then recap succinctly what someone else had to say. Until now, none of us had realized the incredible benefit this would be in allowing her to handle such a difficult part of medical assistance.

As time went on, Nicole continued to watch physician assistants in our one-room office as they learned and recited medical information. She looked over our shoulders as we administered care and spoke with patients. I could see a familiar excitement build in her countenance over the months she worked for us. It reminded me of so long ago in Kathmandu when I felt the burden of medicine begin to beckon me to change my future goals. I didn't push or pry, but deep down, I was excited to see where this new experience might take my daughter.

Soon the time came for her to decide what her future career goals would be. Freshly graduated and packed full to the brim with first-hand experience in journalism, she was torn with this new wonder that medicine held for her. Nicole was incredibly bright. During her studies, she was afforded the opportunity to manage the B-roll shots for the entire Democratic convention during that election cycle. An honor typically reserved for seasoned journalists, Nicole had proven a skill and intelligence that even politicians could easily see. To the common bystander, it made perfect sense for Nicole to take her studies and dive head-first into the vibrant world of broadcast.

But the call to medicine was strong. I knew more than anyone. It had a tendency to interrupt even the most obvious of plans. The job offers for journalism poured in for Nicole, and finally, she sat down with Matthew and me to discuss her next steps.

"I've decided to return to school," she told us.

"What? Excuse me?" I responded.

Why would she go back to school? She had every opportunity to move forward and build a highly successful career.

"Mom, I fell in love with medicine this summer. I want to attend Duke and become a physician assistant like you."

My head was swirling. Of course, I was proud of her decision to pursue medicine, and I had no doubt she would do well. But the memories of Duke and the hellish twenty-four months I spent in that program came flooding back. Here, Nicole was willing to trade a well-worn path to success for a grueling journey into one of the toughest school programs in the country.

"Nicole, that's great to hear, but you don't have any of the sciences. You would need to go back to school and get your prerequisites first. Then you'd need to apply for Duke. I've been there. It's not easy. You may not get in the first time. I didn't."

"I'll go to the junior college and get my sciences, and then I'll go to Duke," she responded flatly. "I will get in the first time. I have no doubt."

Her confidence was unwavering. I knew my daughter was capable of anything, and I was certain she would be an amazing PA. I just feared she was throwing all her eggs in a very tough basket, and I didn't want to see her disappointed. For Nicole, there was no backup plan or second school option. She chose her future, and to her, there was no alternative.

Immediately, Nicole applied to the local college and was accepted. She quickly completed her sciences with ease and then applied for the PA program at Duke. As always, she surprised me with her success and intelligence. Duke accepted her on her first try. When they interviewed her, they asked if her mother was forcing her to pursue this career.

She laughed and responded, "No. I make my own decisions. I watched my mother and fell in love with medicine. I also fell in love with geriatrics. There's a need for this, and I want to be a part of the solution."

Nicole went on to become a magnificent PA. Though it was her brilliance that brought her there, I couldn't help but smile at how our tiny office had been the starting point for her successful career. A lot went into building the practice, but looking back, even more came out of it.

2007–2012

FROM RICHES TO RECKLESSNESS

The years to come were nothing short of incredible. Matthew was requested to serve as medical director for three separate nursing facilities, forcing us to hire more staff to support the patient load. Our practice, Alden Healthcare, eventually acquired more responsibilities, including employee physicals, wound care, and a few house calls if needed. Because of this, we added branches to our practice. Our staff grew to more than fifty employees, and our footprint expanded beyond our community to other areas of the city. Things were simply amazing. Matthew also leveraged his many credentials to become very well respected in the medical community. The work was lucrative, and there seemed to be no stopping us.

As time passed, Matthew and I settled into our new routine of rounds, office visits, and patient care. Our nurses and office staff became family, and the money poured in. Back in 2005, when our small practice consisted of me and Matthew in rented office space within a larger doctor's office, we managed to bring in $125,000 in our first year between both of us. After rent, bills, and payroll, our margins were slim. By now, nearly ten years later, we had pushed the limits and built a medical empire worth more than $2 million in yearly revenue. Our staff was well paid, our pockets were full, and we couldn't help but smile about where our journey had taken us. Neck-deep in rounds and meetings, I'd often pause briefly and go back to the small two-bedroom apartment we first rented while I was at Duke. The long train rides to and from the campus, late-night car rides home, and twenty-four seven studies. I could still taste the ramen noodles I ate nearly every day while reading my textbooks and transcribing my notes. The soft yellow silk of the honors sash I wore on graduation day seemed to stick to my fingers even then. I was blessed, and I knew it.

Matthew, of course, was ecstatic about it all. He had finally found success after years of trying to rebuild what he left behind in Utah. I loved watching him teach and lead, care for and treat. Often, we'd attend the same meetings and even treat the same patients when possible. Matthew's official title was medical director and president of our practice. I served as the clinical director, VP of business development and clinical operations, ands education and lifestyle medicine.

Our practice also extended beyond patient rounds and care. We had started clinical trials for Alzheimer's disease, and members of the press began to notice. One morning, we were contacted by the local news station asking for an interview with Matthew. This was great, except for one small thing: Matthew didn't run them. He was the face of them as our head doctor, but in reality, Nicole and I did all the work. Leading up to the interview, I spent a couple of hours prepping Matthew for what to say and how to answer the questions.

When the interview came, Matthew did well. In fact, he did so well that he took all the credit for the trials. Months of sweat and hard work that my daughter and I had put into the program were forgotten and replaced by Matthew—who really only signed the paperwork at the end. I wasn't bitter, but it didn't sit well deep down. Regardless, it benefited our practice, and the success continued to build.

After a while, I noticed small changes in Matthew's behavior. He was still charming and attentive, but occasionally I saw him tired and somewhat spaced. At times when I'd come to his desk to go over paperwork or discuss a patient, I'd have to catch his attention before he realized I was there. This went on for a while but never seemed to spill over in his patient encounters. But I knew Matthew, and something was off. Often, I'd catch him dosing off during appointments.

With a gentle, barely noticeable nudge to his foot, I'd wake him up, and he'd continue.

I was aware that he continued to refill his narcotic prescriptions for his headaches. In fact, he never really stopped them even since I first found them in Spain years before. But he never showed any of the telltale signs of chemical dependency outside of his routine use. His faculties were sharp, and his mind quicker than ever. But prescription addiction had a funny way of hiding out of sight until the need for a high surpassed the ability to control the effects.

Months later, patients noticed small changes as well. It wasn't until all hell broke loose that we heard the concerns. One of Matthew's patients even mentioned that while he was examining her, his words began to slur ever so slightly, and he appeared to become very drowsy. What alarmed her the most was that he didn't seem to realize it himself.

The staff wasn't aware of any issues with Matthew, and they chalked the occurrence up to a one-off lapse of judgment. Maybe he was tired? When was the last time he had a vacation? They were all good explanations, but unfortunately, I knew the truth. And the truth was much more sinister.

I did my best to keep his problem under wraps, covering for him in meetings and offering up excuses for any more unfortunate side effects. I was good at it for a while, but time and time again, the addiction would break through the curtain and try to complicate things.

One afternoon, I received a call from our pharmacy. "Hello, Ms. Alden. I see that you are coming in to pick up a prescription for hydrocodone. Your chart says you are allergic to it. Do you want us to try and find a replacement with your doctor?"

I was confused. I had never requested this and hadn't talked with my doctor in quite some while. Upon further investigation, I realized that the prescription was written by Matthew and put in under my name to avoid being red-flagged in the system. When I confronted Matthew, he explained it away, giving me his reasons for the mix-up. I knew better. His problem was increasing, and he was starting to lose the battle.

I did what I could to help stop the storm that was approaching. I reached out to Matthew's primary care MD (who was a friend), Dr. Walden, who had been prescribing the narcotics to him for a while. I explained the situation and pleaded with him to stop. Dr. Walden became defensive and assured me that everything was under control. He was convinced that because he managed Matthew's prescriptions personally, there was nothing to be concerned about.

During this time, Matthew and I decided that it was time to purchase our very first home. We had never owned a house before. Because of our financial situation in the earlier years, we could only ever afford to rent. But business was good, and we knew the time had come to build roots in our community. As moving day approached, I went home early to finish packing boxes for the movers. They were scheduled to arrive the next day, and I wanted to make sure all was set. Matthew was supposed to join me as well but hadn't arrived yet.

Hours later, as I was stacking boxes in the front room, I noticed red-and-blue lights flashing through the curtains. I opened them up to see what was happening and saw Matthew's car parked across the street and multiple police cars scattered about. I watched from the window as they walked him through a sobriety test in the street. It was dark, and the flashing lights glared brightly, so I couldn't quite see how he did. My heart sank when I saw Matthew's back turned to me and a police officer snapping handcuffs around his wrists.

Distraught and trembling, I slowly walked down our stairs and approached the police car closest to me.

Once I got the attention of a nearby officer, I asked, somewhat panicked, "What's going on?"

The officer looked at me with a raised eyebrow and crossed his arms, "Obviously, you know."

I had no clue. "No, I don't! Why are you arresting my husband?"

"Ma'am, we followed your husband here after receiving multiple 911 calls about his reckless driving." The officer lifted a hand toward him as he tilted his head in irritation. "It's obvious he is under the influence. We've let him go in the past, but we can't afford to do that this time."

I would find out later that Matthew had been pulled over many times before for reckless driving. He would always convince the officer that he was simply tired. Maybe it was the fact that he was a doctor or well respected in the community, but they'd always let him go. But this time, his actions were too egregious, but seeing the back door of the cruiser close behind him told me what I needed.

My mind was racing, and I felt a panic forming in my chest, like a knot. I whispered under my breath, "We're never buying this house. There's no way he can keep his job after this." I knew that when he got to the jail, they'd perform a toxicology report on him. What on earth would they find in his system? It didn't matter. If it's there—which it obviously was—he'd lose his medical license. The state of North Carolina was strict on this. It would be our undoing.

As the police officers were talking and finalizing their reports, I noticed another car approaching them, and a man walked out. He wasn't dressed like the rest, but the way the officers responded told me he had authority. After speaking to a few of the officers, one of them opened the back door where Matthew was seated and helped him out of the car. In a flash, they mentioned a few words to him, unlocked the cuffs, and set him free.

I had no clue what to think. Just moments before, I was hysterical, trying to make sense of what was happening. I had already written off our new home and wondered what would happen after we were forced to close the practice. Now I watch as a clearly high Matthew walks toward me under his own power. I was both relieved and confused.

When Matthew sobered up and I uncovered the truth behind his spontaneous acquittal, I learned why he escaped jail that night. Apparently, when the officers phoned the station and informed them of Matthew's arrest, they were told that the individual who ran toxicology tests was unavailable that night. There would be no way to pursue charges. The officers agreed to let him go and chalk it up to serendipity. But was it? Or was this divine intervention? Did God work in those mysterious ways tonight? Was it my guardian angel or maybe Matthew's that came to the rescue?

We were able to continue with the purchase of the home and eventually moved the next day. But the stain of what happened was fresh, and I couldn't seem to shake the feeling of hopelessness. I felt as if I was watching a Shakespearean tragedy unfold before my eyes. The mighty hero that had developed in the beginning was slowly unraveling and slipping into madness.

I convinced Matthew to let me control his medicine from that point forward. He reluctantly agreed, but I could tell he struggled with it. Being a doctor for so long, it took a healthy dose of humility to allow his wife and physician assistant no less dole out his portions when it came to prescriptions. But I couldn't see any other way to deal with it. The alternatives would have been detrimental to his career as well as the life we had built.

Though I had control over what he took, I couldn't control what he prescribed for others. As was with any medical office, we had our fair share of patients who were looking to us to supply them with their next fix. Elderly patients had built an unfortunate dependency on narcotics to push away the pain of age and previous injury. During this time, the medical system had not quite evolved to where it was today in the way of monitoring and protecting people from the dangers of controlled substances. It was really up to each individual office and practitioner to do the due diligence.

Unfortunately, being an addict himself, Matthew saw no issue in feeding into the addictions of others. He willingly prescribed heavy controlled substances to his patients upon request with little to no justification. I watched helplessly as more and more addicts sought out Matthew to fuel their fix. To make matters worse, addiction was prevalent in Matthew's own family. His brother was also addicted and relied on Matthew to replenish his own supply often. To this day, I didn't believe Matthew meant harm to those around him. He was an excellent doctor and fully appreciated the Hippocratic oath and our decree to do no harm. But the haze of addiction seemed to blind many of his decisions.

But I did what I could to protect him. I tried my best to keep secrets close and safeguard his license. And I continued to manage his own medications. Having been raised with an alcoholic father in the house, I was adamant about removing the evil of addiction from our home. My father struggled desperately with his dependency. I watched him fail over and over again, losing the many battles he faced with liquor. It was like watching your hero be defeated, then buried. I never knew him not to struggle, and eventually, I watched him succumb to the addiction. At a young age, my father committed suicide to escape the pain of it all.

It was because of this that I simply refused to let Matthew fail too. I knew what addiction could do to a man, and I wanted my family to have nothing to do with it. So I became quite controlling over his pills. Everything was regimented and highly monitored. I constantly checked in and counted pills, set reminders, and asked questions. Of course, this started to wear on Matthew's nerves and ego. But it was all because I loved him and I didn't want to see him fall and because we built our home together. When one fell, the other would inevitably be dragged down with him.

2012–2014

White Dresses and Grandbabies

By 2011, our world took a wild turn, and our family expanded even further. Nicole was getting married! Not one to settle for average, she decided to have a destination wedding back in beautiful Italy. I was thrilled! She had worked so hard to get to where she was, and now she found the most important thing of all: love. Her soon-to-be husband was a delight.

The planning and excitement of it all kept me busy and somewhat distracted from Matthew's increasingly erratic behavior. He still had mood swings, dozing off during patient visits, and showing more and more frustration at me for meddling in his medication. I was unapologetic. I loved him and refused to let this get the better of him.

The day finally arrived, and we flew to Italy to watch Nicole wed in paradise. It was lovely. Surprisingly, we had a rather large turnout. Almost ninety family members and friends from across the nation made the trip. As the song played and Nicole's new husband stood at the front waiting for her to appear, I held back excitement, knowing that Matthew was to emerge, holding Nicole's arm and giving her away at the altar. She had chosen both her dad and Matthew to have the honor.

I was blessed to know how close they became. For nearly two decades, she had grown closer to Matthew than I could have ever imagined. Though she knew he was a stepfather, the bond they created was beautiful. And now she chose him to assist with one of the greatest honors a man could receive, walking her down the aisle. The frustration to a crescendo and I turned to see my beautiful daughter and lovely husband appear.

Nicole was gorgeous. The dress she chose had a simple elegance to it, just like she did. It was almost a pearl-like white with flowing creases at the top, giving way to a flowing, silky dress that was bunched at the bottom. Her veil was lined with ornate stitching on the edges that popped beautifully on her shoulders and then seemed to mesh beautifully as they rested on the dress itself.

She was radiant, and I could see from the front of the audience that Matthew was proud. He smiled from ear to ear as he softly held her arm and guided her to the front of the ceremony. I couldn't help but cry. My sweet family.

The rest of the ceremony was nothing short of amazing. After the "I dos," the sweet couple danced and laughed with their visitors in the reception. The outfit provided by the venue was perfect. We sang and celebrated and drank wine and cocktails to our fill. Then I watched my daughter ride off into the sunset with her new family to enjoy her honeymoon.

Nicole's marriage to her new husband, Robert, was bliss. Both were forward-thinking, driven people and were set on having the best that life could offer. By 2014, Nicole was pregnant with my first grandchild. It was a girl! I was so excited about the idea of having another Nicole. When it came time for delivery, Nicole requested that Matthew attend to welcome baby Lili into the world. We both took turns holding this gorgeous child and fawning over the tired and relieved mother. I had always dreamed of a moment like this but never fully understood how it would feel. Sure, I had ideas, but at that moment, holding my grandchild in my arms, watching my husband fall in love with this baby, and witnessing my grown daughter bring life into the world, there was really only one word that could describe it all: complete.

I was complete. The struggles and sacrifices, sweat and tears that led to a moment like this all seemed to be simply a part of God's magnificent plan. I was thankful for it all. For years I had grappled with

the concept of a mysterious God and His mysterious ways. I recalled
the humility I faced in Nepal, the stress and anxiety I encountered
at Duke, and the worry I felt about Matthew and his struggles. Yet
they all were stepping stones to allowing me a chance to witness this
beautiful moment. He really was mysterious. But He was true. And
this child—this life—was proof.

2015

And It All Came Tumbling Down

Once the dust settled after Lili's birth, the normal rhythm of our life started again. Now there were very few distractions outside of our responsibilities with the practice. Matthew's work and reputation continued to thrive, and I sank my teeth even further into the day-to-day. We were doing great. Money was flowing, and the practice was expanding.

By midyear, Nicole had started planning for Lili's first birthday. I couldn't believe that it had been a year already. The weekend came, and Matthew and I spent the day loving on our grandchild and enjoying the company of friends and family.

Matthew seemed normal that day. Beyond his normal restlessness, he interacted with Nicole and Robert, played with Lili, and participated in the festivities and cleanup. Though his drug-related behavior hadn't necessarily disappeared, I was proud to see that he was functioning at a higher level. He seemed more focused. More resolved. It was as if he had found a new breath to breathe. Though I wasn't sure, I started to convince myself that my persistence in protecting him from the dangers of prescription abuse had something to do with it. I was excited to have my husband back. The party was a success, and after everything was cleaned and Lili was asleep, Matthew and I returned home and prepared for the next week.

The next week at work was typical. By midweek, we were swamped with our routine patients and team meetings. On Thursday, once the day finished, I made it home before Matthew and settled in for the night. Nighttime came, and Matthew was nowhere to be found. I tried calling his cell phone, but it kept going to voice mail. Finally, after a few failed attempts, Matthew answered the phone, and I asked him, "Where are you?"

"I need to stay in the city tonight."

"The city?" I asked. "Why? What's going on?"

"I just need to clear my head. Think about something."

"What things? Matthew, what are you talking about?"

"I just need some time to myself, Addy. Clear my head," he answered again.

It made no sense. What did he need to think through? Everything seemed normal. We hadn't had any major fights or arguments, and to my knowledge, he wasn't abusing his meds. Our marriage had felt sturdy, so I wasn't expecting an affair.

The city (downtown) had been that escape for Matthew back even when we were dating. My heartbeat quickened at the thought of what this could mean. I spent the night searching myself, looking for anything that could have tipped our marriage into the red. Did I say something at Lili's party? Was I too overbearing with his meds? Did something happen at the office today that I was unaware of?

The next morning arrived, and Matthew had stopped answering his phone calls. As I often did in the mornings, I pulled up the business accounts to check on everything when I noticed something alarming. Nearly $70,000 was removed from the account along with roughly $25,000 in random checks. From what I could see, the $10,000 went to various lawyer accounts. I had no clue where the $70,000 was. I started to panic. *Had something happened to our accounts? Was it fraud? Had we been hacked?*

After several more failed attempts to get Matthew on the phone, I decided to call Dina, our bookkeeper. Surely, she would know. The first call didn't go through. Then the second. By the third call, she finally answered, and I asked her if she knew what was happening.

"You know, Addy. I bet he's up to his old tricks again! Doing things without telling us!"

She was probably right, but I couldn't possibly understand why. Regardless, I didn't want any more damage to occur, so I jumped in the car and went to the bank to freeze our accounts.

Once I arrived at the bank, the banker informed me that I had been removed from all our accounts. Not only that, but I no longer had any access to the credit card and was no longer listed as an owner of the company. Just like that, the 45 percent share I had in the company vanished. It made no sense. Who could do this other than the only person with more power over our accounts than me? *Matthew.*

After prodding even further, the bank reluctantly told me that Matthew and Dina, the bookkeeper, had opened their own account together and transferred money from the business into their new joint savings. My head started to swirl. She had just told me she was clueless about it all. What was this new conspiracy?

I left the bank and immediately dialed the credit card company to check on my business card. I found out through them that my card had also been closed. When I asked how, they told me that I had called myself to cancel it just yesterday.

"What do you mean I called? I didn't call!" I shouted.

"Ma'am, I'm sorry, but someone claiming to be you called in and closed the account. And they were able to answer all your security questions."

Dina. She was the only person who knew that information. Not even Matthew would've been able to answer my personal information. Closing a joint account was one thing, but this was something entirely different. She had broken the law, impersonated me, and committed credit fraud. Nothing was beyond this woman.

And nothing was beyond Matthew.

Scrambling now to hold on to every dollar I had remaining, I ran to my personal bank and attempted to withdraw money from the ATM. After a few attempts, I realized that my PIN no longer worked. The teller informed me that the PIN had just been changed. How? Dina would have no problem with the business accounts, but how on earth did she have access to my personal information? I was devastated. I requested to speak to the manager. I needed help. My life was being overtaken before my eyes, and I didn't know how to stop it. The manager was thoughtful and kind and walked me through securing my accounts. She helped me get a new card overnighted to my personal address and put stops in place to avoid any further fraud.

I was shaking when I got back in my car. I whispered to myself, *Okay, God. What next? What is this test?*

It was only the beginning. I was completely in the dark. I made it back home that morning in a daze. Suddenly, there was a knock at the door. I instantly thought it might have been Matthew. *But why would he knock?* I made my way to the door and opened it. A person I didn't recognize handed me a letter and left. Through the plastic envelope window, I noticed a formal letter with my name as the addressee. I opened it and read it aloud to myself. The first sentence read, *"After much thoughtful consideration, Alden Healthcare Ltd. has decided to terminate your employment effective today."*

Matthew had fired me from Alden Healthcare. No warning, no heads-up. The day after he told me he needed space to think through things, the money was gone, I lost access to the accounts, and a stranger appeared at my door informing me I was terminated from the company I cofounded. I was distraught. *How could this happen?* What did this mean? I had no clue what to do next. It was obvious I was no longer an employee, and I was no longer welcome to attend my own company.

I sat at my kitchen table as reality slowly sank in. The walls seemed to tilt forward and move closer. Over and over again, I replayed the last few weeks, looking for any reason this was happening. Matthew was no longer answering his phone, and I was left to fill in the gaps on my own. The story was confusing, broken, and incomplete. Suddenly, between failed calls to Matthew, my phone rang. Nicole. When I answered, she was fuming on the other end.

"Guess what just happened," she started.

My heart sank. *No way. Not Nicole.*

"Don't tell me…," I began.

"Matthew just fired me from Alden, Mom! Did you know about this?"

"No. He fired me too."

This set Nicole off even further. I had wondered if she once thought I was in on her termination. Now it was clear Matthew was getting rid of us. Among the many theories I had tried to piece together, this new information about my daughter's firing pushed one to the forefront. *A coup. Matthew was forming a coup.*

For the next few hours, I tried to contact the office, to no avail. I started grappling with what to do. *Do I go in? Do I stay away? Should I hire a lawyer?* Up until this very moment, I was solely responsible for this company. Matthew was the face, of course, but the oversight for our books, money, and functions was on me. *Where is it now? Who is making decisions?*

The next day was Saturday. I decided to head up to our main office to check on the books and try to get to the bottom of what was happening. I took one of my girlfriends, who was a professional bookkeeper, with me so she could assist. I had no clue what I would find.

We arrived at the office, and I put my key into the lock to open the door. It didn't budge. I tried to shimmy the key and double-checked to see if I was using the right one. Nothing. I looked at my girlfriend, who returned an expression that said what I feared was happening. He *changed the locks.* I walked downstairs and went to the front desk. Pulling out my ID, I requested a security guard come open the door for me. Thankfully, I knew the guards, and they quickly agreed. Later it was revealed that my name had been removed from the list of approved visitors to the office. Had they checked, I wouldn't have made it past the front desk. But he agreed to open the door. He had known me for years and figured it must have been an oversight. I didn't correct him.

The security guard escorted my friend and me back up to the office and let me in the door. Walking into the office, I found Dina knee-deep in the paperwork that had been scattered around Matthew's office. She was obviously looking for something and, at first, didn't notice I came in. After a beat, she quickly turned around and had a startled look on her face. I knew right then that they never wanted me to see what I saw.

"What is going on, Dina? What are you doing here?"

"What are *you* doing here, Addy?" she responded. Her voice had a sinister tinge to it.

"This is my company, Dina. I'm here to check on our books. I'll ask again. What are you doing here in Matthew's office?"

"You are in big trouble, Addy," she answered, ignoring my question. I could see a small grin appear after she said my name.

"Trouble for what?" I answered. Her behavior was almost childish at this point. It felt like she had tattled to a teacher, and I was a fourth grader.

"Oh, you just wait. You will see!"

"Dina, I have no clue what you're talking about. I haven't done anything wrong."

"Oh yes, you have! Just wait. You'll see!"

At this point, Matthew emerged in the doorway. His eyes bulged at the sight of me in his office. Quickly, he regained his composure, and I could see him stick his chest out a tad to try and appear more domineering. "Um, you have to leave now. You can't be here. You aren't part of this practice anymore."

"Really, Matthew? What is going on? What have I done?"

"You will see," he responded. His voice was deepening. "The attorney general will be contacting you soon."

"The attorney general? Really? What does the AG have to do with me?" I answered. I wasn't buying his comment at all.

"You'll see," was all he offered.

Throughout this exchange, Dina kept running her mouth in the background. It felt like a kid in the corner who wasn't invited to the conversation but felt they needed to be heard nonetheless. As Matthew and I continued to exchange short sentences, my friend grew tired of her chirping and turned toward her in a quick rage. "You shut up! This has nothing to do with you!"

On command, Dina pursed her lips and backed away. All that was left was Matthew and me.

"Matthew, we need to talk separately about this. Just me and you. Why don't we meet somewhere off-site and talk through this like adults?" I tried my best to steady my voice.

Matthew folded his arms. "Well, I do need to swing by the house and grab some of my things."

"Okay, great. Why don't we set a date, and you can come by for your stuff? We can talk about this then."

The next week, I got into my car to head to my only remaining job at the free clinic. After I closed the driver's side door, another stranger appeared with another package. This time, it was a larger manila folder addressed to me from a lawyer's office. After signing for it, I opened it up in my car. The first line I read was damning enough: *"Petition for dissolution of marriage from Matthew Alden."*

I couldn't read anymore. *Divorce papers.* First, he took my money, then my company, then my daughter's career. Now he's taking my marriage. *What is going on?* Distraught. That's the only word to describe how I felt. What had happened so quickly that would have caused our marriage to crumble in a matter of a few days? I was numb. It felt as if the air had been sucked out of my lungs.

At this point, I knew I needed to hire an attorney. In fact, not just an attorney—a team of attorneys. I was fighting a war against a well-organized monster and needed assistance. I decided to hire a divorce attorney to protect my assets against Matthew and an employment attorney to try and fight against losing my company. I knew there was something to be said about the way Nicole and I had been terminated. It made no sense!

After doing some research, I heard about Jessica Boulevard and how amazing she was. She had practiced divorce law for nearly nineteen years, and her clients had nothing but amazing things to say about her.

Once I sat down with her, I told her my story. I was emotional and scared. I told her how I felt blindsided by it all, how it made no sense. I found myself unloading on her much like I had been unloading on God up to this point. I must admit, it was nice to have an immediate answer for a change.

I explained how I loved Matthew and couldn't make any sense as to why he would do this to me. When I finally stopped long enough to catch my breath and steady my voice, Jessica looked me squarely in the face. Her eyes were unmoving, and she squinted them slightly with a small sense of defiance and determination. I'll never forget what she said next.

"Addy, I want you to listen to me."

"Okay," I responded feebly. She was very confident about whatever she was going to tell me.

"You married a psychopath," she said flatly.

"What!" I shouted automatically. "No way! He's…"

"Addy, listen," she jumped in. "Everything you just told me describes, by definition, a psychopath. Plain and simple. They are brilliant, charming, and good-looking. And when they are finished with their victim, they are completely finished. No remorse, no sympathy."

The only way to describe my feeling at that moment was shame and embarrassment. She was right. I was so confused. How could I have missed this? I was a medical professional with advanced degrees and a Duke education. I had assisted in diagnosing many diseases and ailments for years, and now suddenly my attorney is diagnosing my marriage. Even more, she was diagnosing my husband.

But it started to make sense. The past decade began to fall into place in my mind, and clarity started rushing forward.

"He's highly credentialed, Jessica," I explained. "He has plenty of certifications, tons of schooling, and he's brilliant."

"This worries me the most, Addy," she responded. "He is used to talking in front of a camera, being a medical researcher and giving his opinions, teaching, etc. He will probably be comfortable in a courtroom setting, having been in the limelight. I'm worried about how you will hold up against him."

I had nothing else at this point. All I had was hope and prayer. "He's really good at his job," I bargained. "But I'm really mad. I'll do my very best. I promise."

A few days later, Nicole and I were given permission by the court to gather our belongings from the main office and officially close the chapter on our employment. I had a few items at my desk and I needed to gather some of my medical books. We worked it out with the front desk to show up, quickly box them up, and leave without a fuss. After talking with the receptionist, and attorneys, we agreed for Nicole and me to arrive at 4:00 p.m. that day, close to closing.

After picking up Nicole, we got to the office at about three fifteen. Traffic was not as bad as we anticipated. We agreed that waiting in our car for another forty-five minutes would be ridiculous, especially since all we were doing was getting *our* belongings, so we didn't ever have to return. When we walked into the waiting room, the office staff was clearly bothered by our early appearance. Somewhat frazzled and very frustrated, they escorted us back to our desks while Matthew was holed up in an examination room with a patient. While Nicole and I gathered our things, I saw through the doorway Matthew frantically waving his arms and pointing in our direction. He wasn't happy we were there.

Close to finishing, my phone rang in my pocket. I pulled it out and saw Jessica Boulevard's name on the screen.

"Hey, Jessica," I answered.

"Addy, where are you right now?" Jessica started. I could hear in her voice that she was concerned about something.

"I'm actually at our main office. Remember, Nicole and I needed to come to get our belongings."

"Addy, listen. I need you to stop what you're doing and leave the office immediately."

My eyes widened. What on earth was going on? "Um, okay, why?"

"I just found out this morning that there has been a restraining order placed against you and Nicole. Matthew's attorney filed it in court without telling me or the judge presiding."

"A restraining order?" I was floored.

"Yes, apparently, Matthew is stating he fears for his life based on some things you and Nicole have said."

"What things, Jessica? What could I have possibly said that would make him do this?"

"That's not important now, Addy," Jessica was growing impatient. "What's important now is that you don't infringe on a pending RO. We will fight it in court with the judge, but right now, you have to get you and Nicole out of there. Matthew's lawyer has informed me that he's notified the cops. They were supposed to be there when you arrived, but it looks like you beat them there."

It was a trap. Matthew wanted me to show up in defiance of an unknown court order. He wanted the court to see me walk off in handcuffs. In a panic, I grabbed what I could and pulled Nicole out the front door. I was white as a ghost. Nicole was livid. On the car ride home, I racked my brain about what I could've possibly said that would merit a restraining order.

Did I say something in a fit of rage when I caught him with D? Was it something he heard Nicole say when she found out?

I came up with nothing. But I knew now what Matthew was capable of, and it scared me of what he may have told the court.

After I hired Jessica, the ball began rolling—quickly. It wasn't a few days after that conversation when she called me to give me an update.

"Hey, Addy, I have some news regarding your case," she began.

"Of course. What's going on?" I had given her everything I knew. I had no clue what this meant. *Were we settling? Was it over before it began? Could I finally get some rest?*

"Unfortunately, it's not good news," she said. My heart sank. "I've received some pretty compelling documents that work against you and Nicole. They are letters from three of Matthew's employees. Apparently, he hired a private investigator who took depositions from all of them. I'll need you to review these documents and respond to what they said about you. You'll need to defend yourself."

I felt defeated. Why would any of our employees say anything like this against Nicole and me? What could we have done?

Jessica emailed Nicole and me the documents after she hung up, and immediately my home office became a crisis center. In the middle of the room, there stood two very large, fold-out conference tables with documents laid out neatly across them. They were organized and categorized. I found myself walking back and forth between them and my computer, searching and identifying documents that supported my defense against their accusations. I would locate my evidence, whether it was an email, receipt, or anything I could hold in my hand that told my side of the story, and I would immediately label it. Then I'd place it next to the pile of evidence against me. Once I had a good response, I then emailed the defense back to Jessica.

I was a mad woman. It was like a fire had been lit beneath me. I started working on the information around six in the morning and would work through midnight most nights. I only took small bathroom breaks and snack breaks, and the occasional fifteen to twenty minutes to hike the hills outside of my house and pray. I would pray, *"God, when will this be over?"*

He said, "Be patient, my child, soon…"

During these moments of solitude, I found myself listening to the song "Fight Song" by Rachel Platten on my headset. The words were perfect for my situation. In some cases, I even added my own lyrics specific to my situation. It helped me through the court battles and long nights:

This is my fight song…
Like a small boat on a big ocean, sending big waves into motion…
I might only have one match that can make an explosion…
And all those things I didn't say are wrecking balls inside my brain…
And I wanted to scream, can you all hear my voice?!
This is my fight song! Take back my life song!
Prove to them that I am right song!
My power is turned on. Right now, I will be strong!
And I don't really care…really care if anyone else believes me…
Because I still have a lot of fight left in me…
Losing friends and colleagues, saying I am in too deep…
All those things I didn't say were wrecking balls in my brain…
This is my FIGHT SONG! TAKE BACK MY LIFE SONG!

I was ready more than ever to prove my innocence. I knew I did nothing wrong, and Matthew would pay for this. And more than that, I knew I wasn't alone. In all His mystery, God was on my side; I was certain of it.

Jessica would immediately send me new evidence gathered from Matthew's side, and I would go to work categorizing and identifying a response. All in all I lost ten pounds in just a few short weeks. I found out later that this was known as the D diet. D for divorce. Believe me when I say that it wasn't a welcomed weight loss.

For the employment attorney, the case was open and shut. Unfortunately, since Matthew held above 50 percent of the company's ownership on paper, he had the right to dismiss me without cause. It was a small blessing in disguise as I could now pour my energy into the divorce and fight for everything I owned. One distraction was gone, allowing me to focus on the other falling pillars that had held up my life for years.

2015

Ex Parte

I still felt the leather sticking to my thighs in the brightly lit courtroom of the local courtroom of the superior court. It was housed in the state office in the city. On either side of the aisle were Jessica Boulevard, Matthew, and his lawyer, Linda Cuthridge. After an announcement to rise, the Honorable Belinda Pile entered from her chambers, seated above her court reporter. Matthew had orchestrated this charade to try and push forward a restraining order against me. *Fear of life due to violent threats* was the reasoning.

To this day, I couldn't help but smirk at the thought of puny ole me striking fear in the mind of the dominating, towering Matthew Alden, especially given that his accusations were as confusing and inaccurate as his need for protection.

After the termination and divorce papers were sent, things snowballed from there rather quickly. Matthew did come by the house a few days later to retrieve his belongings, but with him came a camera-wielding third party, hoping to capture something amiss in my behavior. He reached as far as he could to build up a slam-dunk case against me. If it wasn't misappropriation of funds or embezzlement, then it had to be something more sinister. *A threat of life.*

Robert, Nicole's husband, demanded that he be present when Matthew was to arrive that day. He simply didn't trust that Matthew wouldn't try and stage something for his case or, worse, take things even further. When Matthew came to the door, the man with the camera followed him in, and then another gentleman—a friend of the family—also appeared. It was Matthew's friend and the former sheriff of the area.

Before Matthew could make his way further into the house, I stopped him at the entryway and demanded answers, "Matthew, I need to know what is going on. You told me that you were calling the attorney general. What is this about?"

"You'll find out soon enough," he answered flatly. "They'll be contacting you soon."

"Good," I answered. "Stay right there."

Having worked in high-profile arenas in the area, Matthew and I had built powerful relationships with some of the city's leading officials. One of them was the secretary to the AG. Knowing this, I made my way to the phone and dialed the number on her line. It rang.

Immediately, I noticed sweat droplets form on the brown of Matthew's red face. He was panicking. "Stop, Addy!" he said. "Don't do that. You don't need to call them…"

Just then, the secretary for the AG answered the other line. Matthew continued his incessant interruption as I spoke with her over the phone.

"Hi, Veronica!"

"Hey, Addy! What's going on?"

I saw the color begin to drain in Matthew's voice. He hadn't considered the fact that due to him working directly with the AG's office on an open case in court, I had acquired direction connections to the office and built just as good of relationships with the staff.

"I'm sorry to bother you, but I was wondering if you could do me a favor," I continued. "Apparently, Matthew has submitted a charge against me with the AG, and I have yet to be notified. Could you please look and see if there is something pending against me?"

A moment of shuffling on the other end. The air became tight in the room as Matthew pursed his lips in protest.

"Addy, I have no clue what you're talking about," she answered. It was obvious through the phone that she was very confused.

Matthew spoke out angrily behind me, "Stop it, Addy! You're going to ruin everything!"

"Thank you, Veronica," I said. "That's all I needed to know."

I hung up the phone and turned to face Matthew. I was flushed with anger, and my jaw was clenched, growing sore.

"I can't believe you did that, Addy!" he shouted.

"I just needed to hear it from Veronica, Matthew!" I shouted back. I started walking toward him as I continued, "You've made this whole thing up! What are you trying to pull here!"

To really press in the final sentence, I lifted my hand up and pointed at Matthew's chest with my finger. Suddenly, the man with the camera stepped forward with the lens trained on me and said loudly enough to be heard on film, "Hey! Don't you lay your hands on him!"

My eyes rolled hard in my skull. "Really, Matthew?"

Matthew said nothing, and that was more than enough. The man with the camera and former sheriff followed Matthew and me into the house as he gathered his belongings. They all followed me as if I was a criminal in my own home. I was so glad Robert was by my side as we all paraded through the house like cattle. He gathered his belongings and made his way back out of the house. Robert hugged me as they drove off, and I cried in his arms. That was the last time Matthew ever stepped foot in our home. I was left without contact with him or the company since that moment. And to make matters worse, after I was forced out, the funds were mismanaged, and the company's finances began to turn upside down.

With no one left to oversee the incoming and outgoing, Matthew and Dina were left to run it on their own. It quickly became apparent that one hand had no clue what the other was doing. Matthew, having never been involved in dollars and cents, fully trusted Dina to write checks without sign-off and make decisions she had no business making. For the first time since we opened the doors of Alden Healthcare, the company went in the red. It was like watching a ship I had helped make sink in the ocean while I was left on shore.

To try and keep the ship afloat, Matthew went to the bank to get approved for a loan of $150,000. He put my name down as a coborrower without my consent in an attempt to improve his odds of approval. The ship was burning, and staff, colleagues, and even patients began to notice.

And here we were, ready to face each other for the first time in weeks. I was panicking silently but holding my own. The resilience of my lawyer was the steadiest thing I had felt in a long time. She didn't know it, but I was leaning on her more than anyone else.

When the judge made her way to the seat, you could tell by the look on her face that what she had read in the petition from Matthew's lawyers made no sense. My heart quickened slightly in my chest, but I held steady. *He had no case. It was obvious.*

"Okay, this is the *ex parte* case of Alden. The matter refers to Dr. Matthew Alden and Maria Adeline DeLucca (formerly Alden). This application came from Dr. Alden. For the record, this refers to a domestic violence restraining order that was submitted to the court on or about July 5. I, the judge presiding, was out of the office that day on vacation. Oddly enough, this was the only day I was out of office, and yet that was precisely when this *ex parte* application was submitted." Her eyes quickly turned to face Matthew's lawyer. Ms. Cuthridge was a smallish woman but fierce. I could tell she was typically good at what she did, but whatever the judge was insinuating here revealed otherwise.

I could see a small widening in the lawyer's eyes as the judge's gaze lingered for a second longer before continuing. "Because of that, the case was sent to another judicial officer in my absence. The case pertained to the domestic violence restraining order against Ms. DeLucca as well as a host of other items related to the shared business, Alden Healthcare Ltd., and the return of documents from the house of residence to Dr. Alden."

"Yes, Your Honor," Ms. Cuthridge began. "Ms. DeLucca has in her possession…"

The judge motioned to silence the lawyer with a small wave of her fingers. "Let me finish, Ms. Cuthridge. The presiding judicial officer approved part of this request and dismissed the other half due to a lack of relevancy to the case. Furthermore, Ms. Boulevard came into the court the following week after this application was submitted and informed the court that both parties had been in discussions and this *ex parte* request was submitted without notice from Ms. DeLucca's counsel."

I felt like I was witnessing a movie unfold. Essentially, Matthew's lawyer had tried to fast-track the restraining order and demands regarding the separation from our company while the presiding judge was out of town. Now in front of the judge, and for all to see, there was a three-quarter-inch manila folder full of accusations and demands from Matthew's counsel, and my lawyer hadn't seen it at all. It was as if the iceberg was crumbling all around Matthew, and I was in a rowboat watching it happen.

I caught a glimpse of Matthew as the judge read through the case. He was sweating profusely in his seat. Matthew always sweated when he got nervous. I could see his eyes shift back and forth between his lawyer and the judge.

"What I don't understand here is that I have already vacated the restraining order request made by Dr. Alden against Ms. DeLucca due to there being no true evidence of willful harm on her behalf and the fact that there has been a clear abuse of the concepts of due process regarding this request. Now I see it has been resubmitted by Dr. Alden as an ex parte. Is that correct?"

"Yes, Your Honor. But we understood that the original case was vacated due to additional requests by the court for substantial evidence. We resubmitted…"

"Without notice," the judge interrupted.

Ms. Cuthridge cleared her throat. "Yes, Your Honor. But under the family code, there is no need for a notice regarding an ex parte."

"Oh, I know the code, Ms. Cuthridge." The judge raised an eyebrow and narrowed her eyes. "What I'm saying is that, though this was technically correct, you went out of your way to run around a properly noticed motion."

"Your Honor, it was not my intention…"

"Wouldn't you say that's unprofessional, Ms. Cuthridge?"

"Your Honor, if I may explain," the lawyer continued. Matthew was panicking silently. I could tell. "Both these motions dealt with sensitive files that needed to be returned and an onslaught of disparagement against my client. There was also the domestic violence case that was already in process. I believe the timing is what gives it the appearance of misgivings, but that is not our intention."

"Regardless of your intention, Ms. Cuthridge, you can submit an ex parte with notice to the other side. This is how it's done."

"That was how I originally planned to do this, Your Honor. I noticed counsel we were going to come in on the business issues."

"Then you told her you weren't and still submitted it."

The conversation went on like this for a few more minutes. The furious clicking of the court reporter behind me served as a soundtrack to the dialogue. Matthew's lawyer was obviously cornered, but she seemed to dodge direct answers and skirt outright responsibility for what happened.

Finally, the judge visibly grew tired of the conversation and put an end to her point. It was clear that Matthew's lawyer performed an unethical, albeit allowed, move. As the clock ticked on, our lawyers began arguing the points on either side. By this time, I had been removed from the business account, lost my job, been locked out of all our offices, lost contact with employees and clients, had my credit cards closed, and lost access to money that was rightfully owed. The only thing that I had to my name was what I had in my personal account and the small funds I received from the free clinic. My attorney fees were mounting, and there was simply no way to pay them.

It was also clear that as soon as Matthew had filed for divorce, he took $70,000 from the business account and put it into a joint account with Dina. As my lawyer continued to spell out the events that happened, I sank further in my chair, almost trying to hide from the pain that it all caused me. This was very fresh. Weeks before, I was married, gainfully employed, and happy. Now everything was crumbling around me.

As the minutes droned on, the judge finally approved for Matthew to retrieve confidential mail from our house. We agreed on a third party to come and grab documents from the countless boxes in our garage from Matthew's many cases in which he served as a medical researcher. Before the accounts were totally seized from me, I had managed to siphon off nearly $50,000 to keep myself afloat. The judge slapped my wrist hard in this meeting for that. The money was contested and, in the eyes of the court, government property until it was decided who got what and where.

As we moved into the domestic violence, there was mention of a shotgun at the house. I almost broke my neck when I popped my head up in confusion.

"Ms. DeLucca," the judge said. "Do you have a shotgun locked and loaded under your bed in the house?"

"No, Your Honor," I said. The realization set in. My neck burned hot in anger.

"Then why does Dr. Alden say you have a shotgun under your bed?" the judge asked. I noticed a sigh under her words.

"Because he knew that I had one I used when I hunted with my dad more than thirty years ago. I have not used it since my dad died."

"Okay, and where is that shotgun now?"

"It's at my brother's house. I removed it when Nicole, my daughter, asked me to after my granddaughter was born. *Our grand-daughter.* He knew this." I glared at Matthew. He simply stared back with toddler-like defiance.

"Keep it there, Ms. DeLucca," the judge continued. "We don't need it anywhere near you while this case proceeds. God forbid you'd be tempted."

"Of course, Your Honor," I answered flatly. I was over this. *How ridiculous.*

"And your daughter, Nicole. Is she at the business right now?"

"No, Your Honor. He terminated her as well."

"Okay," the judge quickly rubbed her forehead. "It's not a good idea for her to be there or anywhere near Dr. Alden for the foreseeable future. There are a lot of allegations here that she may have improperly received money from the company and potentially preferable treatment due to her relationship with you. There are also accusations of recent threats allegedly made by her against Dr. Alden."

I had to quit looking at Matthew. I feared if I had, the court would have finally found the threats they were looking for. Matthew had the gall to bring Nicole into this. Apparently, in past conversations, before all hell broke loose, there was talk about life insurance policies between Matthew and Nicole. Essentially, Matthew feared that he'd be, in his own words, "more valuable dead than alive." But he encouraged Nicole to take out a policy on herself. It was then that Nicole mentioned how morbid the conversation of death and money was.

Now that harmless conversation was used as colorful ink to paint a picture of a scared, threatened man. *How dare he.*

Before concluding, the judge stopped the lawyers and turned to Matthew and me. Whatever she said next was only for us.

"Aldens, listen. Emotions are high, and this has now become a lot longer, more expensive, and harder than it probably should have been. But we are professionals. Let us do our job. Calm down and grow up. Let's figure out who owes what and what should be done and move on with our lives. Okay?"

"Yes, Your Honor," I said.

"Yes, Your Honor," Matthew repeated.

"Great. This court is adjourned. We will reconvene for the larger hearing at a later date."

The gavel fell, and the lawyers dropped their professional masks and turned toward their clients to recap what just happened. Now officially, my business—and my marriage—was over. What would happen next was anyone's guess.

2015

Mandates and Mayhem

Court dates and requirements became a circus. Matthew's lawyers looked for reasons to blow certain requirements out of proportion and force higher court costs. It was obvious that money was on their side, and I was burning through the small amount of cash I had saved for myself.

Thankfully, Jessica was thoughtful and devoted to the case. She allowed me to work in her office to help reduce court costs and give me space to stay organized. It also strengthened communication between us so we could stay ready for the next round of shenanigans Ms. Cuthridge and Matthew had planned next.

At one point, I was permitted access to one of our main offices in order to copy documents that would allow me to disprove the allegations Matthew's PI had "uncovered." I agreed to go on my own accord to avoid hiring anyone else. Once the documents were located, there was a third party that would come to do the copying. This was, of course, a court-mandated event, and the exchange was intended to be clean and tidy with no chance of fireworks.

If only that had been the case. When I arrived there in the morning, I waited outside of the office for a while until an entire entourage came to let me in. First, Ms. Cuthridge, Matthew's attorney, arrived. With her was another attorney that I hadn't met yet. Behind them was Dina. She brought her cat with her as well. Why I have no idea. She was so strange! Finally, third-party digital forensics support arrived to assist with the court mandate.

Before I was able to walk in, the office manager asked me to leave all my belongings at the door. I took everything in me not to roll my eyes. Really? Do you think I was going to steal something?

But I kept reminding myself that it wasn't smart to rock the boat. The main one who frustrated the court was Matthew's side of the aisle. I'd lower my head and get through today so I could once and for all dispel these ridiculous allegations.

After the door was unlocked, I walked into Dina's office and spent more than an hour identifying what I could and couldn't move from the office. Once that was done, the lawyers and Dina then spent another half an hour making room in a nearby office for the materials I was going to copy. Everything seemed to move at a snail's pace. I wasn't sure if this was intentional, but I felt outnumbered and very anxious.

The entire time I was there, I was watched. The hired security detail at the front office looked over my shoulder and made sure to remind me with their presence that I was unwelcomed. It was all I could do to keep myself from crying. These were my colleagues. My friends. And now doctors avoided me, and employees glared at me.

Later that evening, I came back with a friend to assist in copying the documents. Once again, we were told to leave our belongings at the front desk. I tried to bargain with this so-called guard that all I had were my shoes, a jacket, and a small radio to listen to the game. I even opened my bag to show her what was in there, but there was no budging. I started to get angry at the presumption.

"Who do you work for?" I asked. "What's your name?"

She refused to answer the question. I told myself that this wasn't right, and I grabbed my camera and took a picture of her to submit later for evidence. *If they want to surveil me, then I'll take a record of them.*

Once I got to the makeshift office Dina had finally prepared, there was another guard standing post outside of the door. I took another picture of her and got her name for the record. I was escorted, observed, and detailed like a prisoner in my own office. My heart was racing. I started wondering if they had set me up for something. *Were these files okay? Did they want to catch me doing something wrong?*

The temperature in the office was stifling. I was sweating along with my friend while we copied the documents. There were no supplies in the office. No pens, no working staplers, stapler removers, or anything that would assist in record finding. I scrambled to find supplies, but when I attempted to leave the office, the security guard announced across the floor that I was leaving as if to alert the manager.

After barely an hour, the guard approached us and told me that I had to leave the office or they would call the police. They accused me of breaching the court order by bringing my friend to help. When the police arrived, they corroborated with security, and I was told to leave immediately. I grabbed what I could, and we exited.

I was a mixture of emotions. Sad, mad, scared, anxious. I didn't know what had happened. All I knew was I was intimidated once again. Dripping in sweat and fighting tears, I made my way to my car and left for the evening with the documents I could spare in the back seat.

As my friend and I drove home that night, we sat in silence for a while, taking in what just had happened.

She finally blurted out, "Addy, I am so sorry you are going through this is a f——king shit show! You don't deserve this! You made this man everything he is today."

She wasn't one to mince words. Thank God she was driving because the tears rolled down my face, and I was so choked up I couldn't even answer her back.

Days later, Jessica, my lawyer, described the situation in detail to the court. Judge Pile was furious.

"What is this? A circus?" she shouted. I'm not entirely certain, but I felt like I could see Matthew's lawyer cower slightly with the question. "The ex parte clearly states that Ms. DeLucca had every right to bring someone with her to assist with copying. I don't understand why the files weren't ready and why there was such a spectacle made for this to happen. Do you not want to settle this, Dr. Alden?"

"Yes, Your Honor," he feebly responded.

"Then do what you agree to do!" Judge Pile continued. "Stop with the antics and show. You are wasting time and money with this behavior. Counsel, I'd advise you to fix this before it snowballs further."

With the small victory, I felt a grin tug at the sides of my mouth. *She's getting it,* I thought. Jessica didn't say anything else about it after that. We moved on to defend against the other attacks.

Once the court was adjourned, I left that day still overwhelmed by everything, though. It was back to pulling the all-day shift in trying to defend my name.

As the months droned on, the accusations from Matthew's side of the aisle seemed insurmountable. From reinforcing this asinine story of violent threats and shotgun-clad madness to misappropriation of funds and embezzlement. He pulled out all the stops and did his best to paint a sinister picture of me.

Most of the insults bounced off easily. I was obviously not a violent person. I had never even imagined hurting Matthew or anyone for that matter. All the court had to do was look at me and surmise the same. Both physically and financially, I was in no position to try and dominate Matthew or his counsel.

But the sting of those letters that Jessica showed me from Matthew's employees—our employees—lingered. After weeks of truth seeking, I finally answered every complaint and accusation and backed it up with hardcore proof. Though I was confident that I was clear of any wrongdoing, the stench of mutiny and betrayal hung over me like smog.

Weeks after the ex parte hearing had adjourned, Matthew and I found ourselves facing each other in court again. It was my turn to answer the emails and employee accusations and for the court to decide if what was said against me held weight.

Once again, the bailiff announced the entrance of Her Honor, Judge Belinda Pile. As she made her way to her chair, in her hand was a folder of pages. A few corners of the files were crooked in a pile, revealing the font shape and color. Once I saw the lime-green characters peeking out among the black, I knew they were my responses. I wanted there to be no questions when she read my answers, so I chose a font that would stick out clearly. From across the courtroom, I could see the answers boldly, so I had no doubt she didn't miss a word.

"This court is now in session. Today we are discussing the case of Alden v. Alden regarding the dissolution of marriage and allocation of assets regarding Alden Healthcare Ltd. as well as the cause for damages against either party as represented in their cases. Counsel, you may proceed."

"Thank you, Your Honor." Jessica moved to the side of her table as she picked up our own file of the same responses. "I'd like to call attention to Ms. DeLucca's responses regarding the accusations of three employees within Alden Healthcare Ltd. Employees hired and managed by both Dr. Alden and Ms. DeLucca who accused my client of wrongdoing, including creating hostile work environments, illegal and unnecessary monitoring of associates, and overall menacing and abusive behavior."

"Yes, I have read the responses from Ms. DeLucca." The judge squinted her eyes in thought as she picked up the file.

"Thank you, Your Honor," Jessica continued. "Dr. Alden's counsel submitted for evidence three letters that employees had written painting a negative picture of Ms. DeLucca. The responses we provided clearly articulate no wrongdoing on behalf of Ms. DeLucca and furthermore provided clear evidence disproving such accusations. In addition to this evidence, there were also twelve more letters provided by other employees of Alden Healthcare Ltd. that offer glowing and positive examples of Ms. DeLucca's management and leadership style while employed at the clinic as well as personal character references that completely contradict the accounts provided by Dr. Alden's counsel. Should I read the accounts in detail?"

"No need," the judge answered quickly. "I've read the statements. It's obvious to me that Ms. DeLucca has more friends than enemies in the office. And the evidence provided by Ms. DeLucca to back up her responses to the accusations hold weight."

I felt a large weight lift from my chest. The judge appreciated my responses. Even though it was obvious we weren't close to finishing, I still felt slightly vindicated by it all. But the pain of what those three employees, whom I thought were my friends, wrote about me was still there. I slipped a quick glance toward Matthew to see how he took the judge's remarks. He sat quietly, stoically. Besides his telltale sweating, he didn't seem bothered at all.

I couldn't help but shake my head. *Why, Matthew?* I wondered silently. *What did I do to you for you to try and ruin my name like this?*

But there were no answers. Somewhere, deep in his mind and soul, he had made up his mind to see me ruined. And I had no clue why.

The court appearances continued for weeks. I felt as if I lived in that leather chair behind that large wooden desk. After many courtroom dates, the gray pitchers of water and small glasses in the center of the table became too familiar for their own good. For hours, I'd occupy my mind tracing out the small details of the glass and looking for new fingerprints or smudges. Days and weeks blurred together as more and more insults and responses were lobbed from either side of the aisle like bombs in a battle. And no matter who won the fight, we all walked away bruised and battered.

After the judge awarded me alimony due to my termination from the practice, the checks were yet another struggle I couldn't seem to win. Whether it was not receiving them from Matthew on time or having them bounce after the deposit, it became clear that he had no intention of paying me what was owed. After weeks of back and forth, Jessica stepped in the middle and involved the court.

With yet another appearance with Judge Pile, it was decided that Matthew would provide a cashier's check on each appointed date, provided by his lawyer's office, to my lawyer.

I couldn't help but roll my eyes when the verdict was decided. Here, this man had squandered my money for years. Taken cash advances from credit cards he didn't own, stole opportunities from my own daughter to fund God-knew-what in the main office, and left me broke and stranded in Spain after promising to fund the vacation, and now amid court-mandated alimony, he was doing it again.

But I was less frustrated with him and more disgusted with myself in it all. Why did I spend so many years trusting this man? Why had I not seen him for who he truly was?

Suddenly, while sitting in that leather chair, a distant memory flooded my mind. I saw the betrayal in Dr. Ellis's eyes as he leaned in toward me in that hospital hallway.

"One day, Addy. One day, you'll regret following Matthew," he said.

Boy, was he right. That day had finally come. I regretted so much of it. Yes, there were beautiful moments, but looking back over it all, I now clearly saw all the mess that was covered by a thin layer of passion and love. Tears welled in the corner of my eyes as I witnessed the beautiful moments of our relationship: the passionate lovemaking in Barcelona, the beautiful glass plaque he gave me after graduating from Duke, and the countless dinners and toasts made as our business grew. I loved this man. I gave this man all of me.

And now he was doing everything he could to take it back.

2016

Changing of the Guard
and Finding Closure

The dust storm that was our fight in court started to settle after Matthew fired his counsel. His lawyer, Ms. Cuthridge, had shown a rather large ineptitude with his case, racking up an obnoxiously large bill and showing multiple, frankly embarrassing, missteps in front of Judge Belinda Pile.

After the court stepped in to require alimony to be paid officially, it was obvious that Matthew ran out of funds to keep paying her. Jessica, my lawyer, was informed that his new counsel was a well-respected lawyer named Ignacio Garcia.

"Addy, he's really good," she told me. "Good for Matthew, but also good for us."

"How so?" A good opposing lawyer didn't seem to be a plus in my case.

"Well, he'll take care of Matthew, but he also won't tolerate the nonsense that Matthew has been trying to get away with," Jessica explained. "I really respect him. He will work hard to finally close this case out and get things settled. This is a good thing."

I was cautiously optimistic. I definitely didn't have the money to keep fighting this case, and hearing that an adult would finally step in and drive Matthew's side of the house was encouraging.

Thankfully, Garcia held true to his reputation. Suddenly, court appearances became less frequent and more organized. After meeting with the judge, it felt, for the first time, that boxes had been checked and mileage had been made of our case.

Judge Pile came in and threw down a huge stack of documents that appeared nearly one foot tall and looked at Matthew and his attorney.

"Dr. Alden, you and your former attorney have wasted this court's time," she began sternly. "You have presented all this so-called evidence, and nothing has been proven against Mrs. Alden. Therefore, I am requesting you pay all the court fees and her attorney fees."

Matthew's new attorney cleared his throat and attempted an objection.

Before he could begin, Judge Pile cut him off, "I have made my ruling. I understand both parties have decided to go into mediation rather than divorce court."

Both attorneys answered, "Yes, Your Honor."

"Then court was adjourned. I will see you all in mediation two weeks from today."

Mediation was the best-case scenario. This way, we would sit together with both our representatives and officially decide who got what and how we could move on once and for all. When Jessica brought it up to me early that week, I immediately said, "Yes." No more long sessions with gavel bangs and *he-said-she-said*. Just plain ole *"You get this"* and *"She gets that."*

"Let's do it," I told her.

The date was set, and Matthew and I worked individually with our lawyers to discuss what we wanted to walk away with after it was all said and done.

2016

Mediation and Closure

When the day arrived, we sat across from each other in the judge's chambers, surrounded by legal counsel and a court reporter. Judge Pile brought out a large whiteboard with a house in the middle, our house. Then on either side was my and Matthew's name. On the far side was a list of assets that summed up our whole life together. Cars, companies, banks, and materials. I found it unsettling that the years of love and devotion I gave to him had been boiled down to a list of purchased goods. But nevertheless, here we were.

To kick things off, the judge put under each of our names a figure that represented *earning potential*. This was how much money we were capable of making in a given year by ourselves. The gap between us was astounding.

Under Matthew's name was nearly half a million dollars for the year. Undermine was a fifth of that. Suddenly, the baseless claim that Matthew had for wanting to retain everything for himself was laid bare. He effectively wanted to leave me with nothing I had helped create.

For three hours after that, we went through each line item individually. Our lawyers spoke on our behalf and used our predetermined list as a reference. I sat back, mostly silent, watching the past decade of my life be reduced to barter. I somehow tuned it all out. I was silently saying the Hail Mary and asking God to help me get through this. Then I heard him… *"Be patient, my child. You're almost there."*

I heard Jessica say, "Addy, are you okay with this?"

Somewhat startled, as if I wasn't even present, I quickly had to pull my thoughts back to the whiteboard a read what was being presented to me. "Yes," I responded, and so did Matthew, much to my surprise.

When it was all said and done, I left that day with the house, five years of mandated alimony (normally half of marriage, which should have been 7.5 years), and retention of all the patents we developed together. Matthew walked away with the business. Frankly, I was fine with that. Since being ousted, the business had flipped to the red for the first time since we opened. Matthew was losing money, patients, and employees due to mismanagement and distrust. Payroll checks were bouncing, and invoices were left unpaid. *Good riddance.*

The judge sighed a deep sigh of relief once the whiteboard was full. The court reporter read back final notes, and a soft, cheerful gavel fell, putting an end to months of struggle and despair.

Jessica and I gathered our belongings and walked through the parking lot toward our vehicles. The warm air felt like a blanket, cozy and soft. For the first time in months, I noticed every detail of nature, the smell of the air and the sounds of birds and cicadas. I even found rest in the busy noises of the nearby highway.

I was free. As I approached my car, I felt Jessica lock arms with me and lean on my shoulder. When we got to my driver's door, she put her hands on my shoulders and straightened me toward her firmly but softly.

"Addy, listen to me," she said. Her eyes were focused, and I saw that familiar intensity she had had since we met. "Never, in my wildest dreams, did I imagine this thing working out for you as it did."

I started to cry softly.

She continued, "Judge Pile worked magic for you in there. It's a miracle."

She was right. It *was* a miracle. And though I was so thankful for Judge Pile and Jessica for all they did throughout this journey, I couldn't help but recognize another party. The mysterious and somewhat elusive figure that had never abandoned me through any of it. And though there were many times I scratched my head and asked that same old question over and over again, *"What mystery are you doing now, God?"* He carried me through it. He did it again.

And I was thankful.

2017

CATHARTIC CONCLUSIONS

Once it was settled, I was settled. After that wonderful day in Judge Pile's chambers, I set my eyes on my own future and carved out a new path to follow. I found a wonderful employer who gave me plenty of time off to tie up the loose ends of my divorce and navigate the last few court dates, including the mediation. From there, I, once again, began to thrive in my profession.

I eventually found a new place to live in Arizona. Though the climate trade was rather alarming, I knew the distance from old memories would do me well. Word got out in my new community, and my list of patients grew substantially. Life had new meaning.

Nicole also thrived. After being terminated, she never did see Matthew again, even throughout the trial. It was just too hard. She had given this man so much love and respect for so long. To her, it was as if the rug had been taken out from underneath her, and she was left bruised and broken from it all. I respected her decision. I myself had no plans to see him again either.

Once the dotted lines were signed, we parted ways respectfully, him back to his dying companies and me to my new beginnings.

About a year later, I received a phone call from a dear friend. She was employed by our main office and called to let me know she had left Alden Healthcare a month prior. She wanted to clear the air and apologize for not stepping up during the trial.

"Addy, I wasn't there for you," she said. "A lot of us were told not to say anything. That the case was pending, and we would be in legal trouble if we spoke out."

This didn't surprise me. After all, we were told the same thing by the judge.

"Honestly, it's okay," I responded. "What's done is done."

"Well, I figured I'd let you know what happened after you left."

I hadn't really wanted to explore more about the company, but now that it was done, a little reveling was in order. She filled me in on what took place.

Apparently, paychecks went unpaid, and three of the employees, two of whom had spoken out against me during the trial, were now suing Matthew for unpaid wages. There was a date set and rumors that I would be asked to come to testify on their behalf.

"It's only rumored at this point, so not sure if you will have to. But I wanted to give you a heads-up."

Turns out, she was right. A few days later, I received a subpoena to appear in court as a witness for one of the former employee's cases. The date was a week away, back in North Carolina.

The plaintiff? *Dina.*

I wanted nothing to do with this woman after what she did. She willfully conspired against me and aided Matthew as he ousted me from my own company. A family friend and employee turned against me and did her best to bury me. But it was a subpoena, and I was powerless.

The next week I showed up to the trial and sat in the witness chair. The questions were very basic, mostly against Matthew. I made sure to answer only what was needed and provide just the details that were requested. Nothing more.

After the session adjourned, I walked down the courtroom steps and saw Dina walking out of the separate doorway with her lawyer. There was a brief, movie-like moment where we caught each other's attention. She stared at me from across the steps for only a moment.

She was ashamed. I could tell. It was somewhat of a satisfying feeling to see her facial expression. It was a subtle mix of frustration and regret.

That was good enough for me. Had she even wanted to apologize, I wasn't interested in hearing it. Seeing that she had her own struggles due to the mess, she helped make all the retribution I needed. I returned back home to Arizona the following morning and carried on with my simple, happy life.

Weeks later, as I was preparing for another day in the office, I scrolled through my Facebook account as my coffee was brewing in the kitchen. It was mindless for the most part, just a way to speed up the minutes it took to get my morning cup.

Suddenly, as I scrolled down, I saw a large photo of Matthew's center screen. It wasn't a headshot or profile pic, though. I had unfollowed him on everything. No, this was a part of an article shared by another mutual friend, and the photo was an unflattering mugshot. The headline was damning: EMBATTLED DOCTOR GETS 10 YEARS FOR SEXUAL BATTERY.

I felt the blood rush from my face as I zoomed in on the words *sexual battery*. Almost as if on cue, my phone began to ring. It was Nicole.

"Mom, have you seen it?" she began. She was also a mutual friend of the one who shared it.

"I'm looking at it now. What happened?"

"Have you read the article?" she asked.

"Not yet," I answered.

"I talked with Mandy in North Carolina," she explained. "Apparently, one of the office receptionists had filed a sexual harassment complaint against him a month ago. No one heard about it because it was under investigation. From what they are saying, he assaulted her in his office during a quarterly review. He pled not guilty yesterday but was found guilty and was sentenced to ten years."

"Who was it?" I asked, not that it mattered.

"I don't know. The article won't say, and no one from the office is talking about it. I've only heard from a few friends who know some patients from there still."

"Oh my god," was all I could say.

"Mom, it gets worse," Nicole continued.

"How?"

"Well, apparently, whoever this was said that the abuse had been happening for two years."

It took everything in me not to drop the phone on my kitchen counter. The room started swirling as I grappled with what Nicole had just told me. Not only was Matthew trying to destroy my life and reputation, but he was also sexually accosting our staff. We were still married. We were still happy. I was still his, and he was still mine.

And he was harassing a woman I knew.

I hung up with Nicole and called out of work. My boss was understanding as he had heard through the grapevine what had happened. I decided to get out of the house and go for a hike to try and clear my mind. Nature and fresh air were some of the best ways I made it through the court appearances and torture of my divorce. I knew I needed to use them both now.

I dressed warmly as the Arizona air started growing crisp. Near my new home was a nice, easy climb to the top of a hill. I had climbed it before and loved the views at the summit. I wasn't looking for a challenge, just an escape.

The climb took an hour. Once I got to the top, I found a small clearing that overlooked the town below and laid out a blanket. My mind was racing. I had been somewhat distracted by the news as I focused on my steps and surroundings up the hill. But now I had no distractions other than the views, and they weren't enough to keep my imagination from wandering off. I began to wrestle with the same questions I had carried throughout it all. *Why, God? What mystery are You trying to show me here? Why did You allow this all to happen to me?*

It was selfish to think of myself considering the woman he had assaulted. But I couldn't help it. Just when I thought I was rid of him for good, he had reinserted himself back in my thoughts, back in my life. I felt like I couldn't escape it.

Deep in thought, I absentmindedly scanned the mountainside below. I wasn't looking at anything in particular, just somewhat lost in thought and exhaustion.

Suddenly, from the corner of my eye, something seemed to glisten from the reflection of the sun. I shook out my questions to God and looked to see what it was. In the thicket of grass and weeds, I saw a small silver bracelet with a charm on it. The charm was polished and reflected the sunlight beautifully.

I reached over and grabbed it, lifting it close to my face while I inspected it. This spot was popular with the locals. Young people frequented it often during the summers and when school was out in the evenings. The chain was small and cheap. It was clearly not real silver but rather coated with a thin layer as some of it had worn from the elements, revealing a bland gray metal beneath. The charm was shaped like a heart and had a clasp on one side. It was large enough to have something inside. Maybe a picture or drawing.

I pulled at the clasp and struggled to open it. It was clearly weathered and corroded. Whoever this was had left it for a long time. I finally opened the charm and lay bare its secrets in the sunlight. It was a quote beautifully written with dark-red letters.

I brought you through it, and you listened.

—God

I immediately began crying. For decades I had asked Him, "Why?" For years I had wondered what the mystery had been. Why had He allowed the struggles and pain of so many problems, detours, and disappointments? And up to this point, the questions had gone unanswered.

It was clear now. The heartache, misery, shame, and deceit. The abandonment, manipulation, and lies. Every last one of them had given way to strength, resilience, and overcoming. I was no longer a victim. I was a victor. And He was reminding me that now I could use it for good.

But now, on the very day of Matthew's sentencing, I finally received the answer I had been looking for. The locket reminded me. I listened to His words, and now I knew why He kept saying, "*Be patient, My child.*" I finally had my redemption. I was free of the bondage of Matthew that had tormented me.

I closed the locket back up and carefully placed it in my hoodie pocket. With a deep breath, I took in the scenery one last time with fresh eyes and made my way back down the hill.
My new life continued. The mystery had been solved.

Will Addy find true love again? Will the pain
of past trauma ever really heal?

What happens next may surprise you. Stay tuned.

Lili

About the Author

For years, Alex Russo heard stories from friends and family about their search for love and their forever partners. Over cocktails, laughter, and tears, they talked of wedding bells that always ended in ugly divorces. Alex would keep asking the same question, "Why won't they listen?" They were falling for the wrong men over and over again and never understood why. All they needed to do was step back, slow down, and listen for the voice of God. That's precisely what this book is about. It's a cautionary tale about choosing the right person and hearing the right voices even when most refuse to do so.